Divine Love Mediumship

Explorations in Divine Love

Divine Love Mediumship

Explorations in Divine Love

The rights of the original author are asserted:
Albert J Fike, of Gibsons, B.C. Canada

Published by the Divine Love Sanctuary Foundation,
Gibsons, B.C., Canada.

For more information go to:
http://divinelovesanctuary.com

© Copyright August 2018.

Revision 1.4

ISBN: 978-0-359-00805-6

Cover Design: Raphael Legros

This is the second volume in the series: "Explorations in Divine Love." The first volume, "The Quiet Revolution of the Soul" was published in August 2016.

Dedication

Geoff Cutler has been a stalwart of the Divine Love movement. Having met him in 2012, he has become an ardent supporter of my work and a good friend. He has supported Divine Love mediums the world over and continues to encourage us in our work. There are few who have put in such consistent effort to get the truths of Divine Love out into the world. He deserves our thanks and love for being the bright soul that he is in a world that is often deaf to the words of truth.

If I speak in the tongues of men or of angels, but do not have love, I am only a resounding gong or a clanging cymbal. If I have the gift of prophecy and can fathom all mysteries and all knowledge, and if I have a faith that can move mountains, but do not have love, I am nothing. If I give all I possess to the poor and give over my body to hardship that I may boast, but do not have love, I gain nothing....Paul, 1 Corinthians 13:1-3

Preface

This is not a book on how to receive typical communications from Spirits. Rather, its focus is on receiving an essence of God called Divine Love and with a concerted effort on developing the faculties of our souls, the gift of Divine Love mediumship with Angelic support may come about. Though all mediums need to know certain things about the art of spirit communication, the object of Divine Love mediumship is to open up the possibilities of communication with very high and soul-lit spirits which we call Celestial Angels. Communication with spirits in the spirit spheres does not necessarily require that the medium has a well-developed or light-filled soul, and many spiritualists are not necessarily God-centered. Their primary goal is to prove the existence of life after death and possibly bring some comfort to grieving loved ones back on earth and they perform a great service to humanity by utilizing their gifts in this way. Divine Love mediums, however, need not focus on this form of spirit communication per se because connecting with highly evolved souls or Angels requires a somewhat different approach. There are higher standards and levels of spiritual development required for one to become a Divine Love medium. It is unlikely to bring fame and fortune, but a much higher reward is gained with the awakening of one's soul in Divine Love. Inner joy and peace comes with this journey. Connection and communication with Angels has in itself deeply spiritual rewards. Access to the wisdom of the Angels will propel you forward upon your spiritual journey. Being a channel for the Angels to communicate with others is a beautiful way to serve humanity. With effort and persistence, discovering the joys and benefits of becoming a Divine Love medium brings a dimension and depth to life that is incomparable to other paths towards spiritual enlightenment. If you sense an attraction and curiosity as to what this journey entails, it is my sincere hope that you will find some inspiration within these pages.

Al Fike

August 4th, 2018

Contents

Chapter 1

Beginnings

Building a grounded and thorough understanding of what is needed in Divine Love mediumship requires a soul awakened to some degree by the blessing of this Love. When the consciousness of the soul and the spiritual knowledge of the material mind come together in a firm and grounded way, the door to mediumship can be opened. Gifts of spirit communication can be demonstrated in a variety of ways. Trance mediumship is but one form. Clairaudience and clairvoyance are considered valid tools of spirit communication. Material mediumship represents yet another form of communication. Many are capable of receiving visions and impressions while others can communicate by using automatic writing. Many avenues may be taken and some people are able to communicate utilizing a variety of these gifts. Each of us possesses at least one of these gifts. In the journey of developing your unique abilities to bring through messages from the Angels, the opening of the soul faculties through receiving Divine Love fosters and organically develops your unique abilities. It is an incremental process and one that must not be rushed.

Since there are many forms of mediumship practiced in the world, this type of communication can be easily confused with others. Only Divine Love mediumship requires the soul to be opened and developed by receiving the Divine Love. It is necessary because the faculties of the soul, which are ignited by receiving this blessing, are necessary for consistent and profound communication with Celestial spirits. Since Celestials are indeed high spirits who have been transformed completely by the Love of God, in order for them to make contact with mortals on earth there needs to be an activation of the laws of attraction to realize connection. They are only capable of making the necessary rapport for communication with like souls on the earth plane because they cannot circumvent the laws of attraction. If one is to attempt to connect and communicate with Celestials, then the individual needs to have some Divine Love in their soul.

Unfortunately, there are some mediums who claim to be in contact with Jesus and other high Celestial spirits but openly admit to no knowledge or practice of receiving the Love within their souls. In this instance, the possibility that they are having frequent conversations with and messages from Jesus and other Celestials is improbable. Yet highly evolved souls like the Celestial Angels are capable of many things, so one cannot rule out completely this relationship with a medium that is not cognizant of Divine Love. Lack of this knowledge will certainly repress the main message of Celestials which is in receiving God's Love in order to obtain the rebirth of the soul.

Consequently, if a medium has no prior knowledge or practice of receiving within their souls the blessing of Divine Love, the likelihood that messages pertaining to soul development in this way will be at best distorted. Such are the laws of communication and rapport. If there is little or no prior knowledge of some truth, it is very difficult indeed for a spirit who wishes to convey that knowledge through a medium to do so with any clarity and success. Of course, there are many in the

2

world who have experienced the Divine Love and possess it to some degree, yet have no conscious understanding of it. Realizing an open and consistent communication with Celestials may be possible in this case but a sustained connection is difficult at best. The angels do try hard to make contact with mortals, however, and this can be accomplished with the openness and desire of a mortal to invite this connection. The law of desire works in our favor in this regard. The picture though, is incomplete without some knowledge and activation of Divine Love. Hence knowledge, faith and prayerful perseverance brings the results that one needs for the development of Divine Love mediumship.

The goal of this book is to share both knowledge and a step-by-step process of how to go about developing Divine Love mediumship. It is not an overly complicated journey and this book is not designed to burden you with intellectual language and complex details. Instead, its purpose is to inspire and support you on this incredible life-altering path of opening the faculties of your soul in order to awaken the gifts of communication with Celestial Angels. Using your intuition combined with innate psychic and soul faculties, you will find an avenue towards your own unique gifts. With a firm grounding in prayer for receiving Divine Love, one can move forward in developing some form of Divine Love mediumship. Timing is important as integrating the changes that this phase of soul development brings can be daunting and dynamic.

One must be fully prepared and committed to the journey. Shortcuts cannot be taken unless you are ready to invite a great deal of confusion and contradiction as there are numerous spirits from the many spirit spheres who are very keen to use an open medium to communicate whatever their agenda dictates. Cautious, slow and steady progress will win the race. Deep prayer and yearnings for the inflowing of God's Love is pivotal. A desire to serve God as a channel of His Love and Truth must be your primary motivation. Having a deep faith in yourself and in the process will carry you to your goal.

This message from Jesus received by H, who resides in Ecuador, gives us some key insights in how to begin.

Hearing your inner voice

> *Spirit: Jesus, August 17th, 2001*
>
> *I am here, Jesus.*
>
> *I have observed you as you passed the whole day thinking of the trance message that I delivered last June; and above all, the part where I spoke about the internal voice, referring to the question by Geoff, impressed you very much. You have wondered if you, too, could develop this ability - the ability to hear "your internal voice" clearly. I write "your internal voice" between quotation marks, because, in fact, it is not your voice, it only sounds in your interior, but it is a voice of external origin - it is our voice, the voice of the spirits.*
>
> *All people have the ability to perceive this internal voice, and in fact, everybody hears it, but in most cases, they don't listen to it. And there are three reasons for this to happen. First, it is difficult to distinguish it from your own thoughts, because we, the spirits, have to use the instruments that the human puts at our disposition, that is to say, his or her mind. And in that mind, we formulate the answers or suggestions that we wish to convey. Of course, this voice doesn't ring distinctively, and since it originates in your brain, it is part of your mind, the same as your own thoughts are part of your mind, with the one exception that this voice was implanted into you, impressed upon you, as right now I am impressing you with these thoughts.*
>
> *How are you able, then, to distinguish if what you*

perceive, feel, and "hear" comes from us, and are not the machinations of your own mind? I admit that this is difficult, but in this same moment you can already give yourself the answer: Our voice arrives accompanied by certain sensations; you have the impression that you are not "hearing" it in your head, in your brain, but you're rather feeling something, which is formulated in your chest, in your heart, and is a very similar sensation which you perceive when the Love flows into you, transmitting the impression of your chest being contracted, but a pleasant, happy sensation. You feel the same happiness now, and in fact, I can assure you that you are experiencing the inflowing of this Great Love that the Heavenly Father grants us in his infinite Kindness.

As I have said, our coming and communicating is accompanied by certain sensations that allow you to realize that what you are feeling, and the information that you are receiving, is not information that your own mind is formulating, but is something that comes from outside - from the world you still ignore - from the wonderful world of the spirits.

I have explained to you the first reason, why people don't perceive, or why they refuse to perceive, this kind of communication: Simply, they confuse it with their own fantasy. But there is another reason. Imagine the soul like a radio receiver. You can still remember those old apparatus, which, together with the transmission of the sounds, also transmitted a boisterous background crackling. You can sometimes hear this phenomenon even today. When you drive a car with the radio turned on, and as you move out of the reach of the broadcasting station, in the same way the noise increases, interfering with radio reception, making it more and more difficult to understand the speaker.

In some way, this is what also happens with the soul. The

soul has a potential power of reception, of perceiving our voices, of being tuned in with the world of the spirits. But besides the work of tuning in to the "radio station," that is, of elevating your spirituality, of getting ready with spiritual thoughts, primarily of a corresponding sustained attitude, there are other factors intervening with the clear reception of our messages and our guidance.

You live in a noisy, materialistic world, which scarcely leaves you time to devote yourselves to what is much more important because it is potentially eternal: the development of the soul. Well, this is not exactly true, because, yes, there is time, all the time in the world to do this, but the distractions and the amusements are so great, that people don't take the time to dedicate it to the spiritual things. We could say that this atmosphere acts like an extremely strong background noise. Their upset thoughts are like the deafening waves of the ocean, like the boisterous surf, which covers our intent of entering into contact with you.

Therefore, you have to work to make the volume of this background noise lower, and this is not difficult to do. Take your time; retire from this world from time to time. For this purpose you don't need enter a monastery, no, just retire to a calm, silent place, a separate room, a corner in the forest or in the near-by park where you may stay awhile all alone, all alone with us and with God. You will be surprised how quickly your perception of our guidance will increase.

When I lived on earth, the world was calmer; noisy, yes, but we had more moments for contemplation, at least those of us who enjoyed the invaluable gift of freedom. As a boy, when studying the Hebrew Scriptures, many times I felt that interior voice very clearly, and I was always filled with a great deal of happiness.

As we informed you in other messages, I was born without sin; that is to say, I didn't have those encrustations which deform the soul, and this is very important to take into consideration. These encrustations are the third reason, why you, many of you, have so much difficulty in receiving our guidance. You could compare these encrustations with an insulating layer muffling our voice, and this, in combination with the aforementioned background noise, makes the perception of our advice and messages almost impossible.

Therefore, besides retirement and meditation, there is another work that you have to do in order to improve reception. You have to remove, to tear away and eliminate, these encrustations. And there is only one instrument which serves this purpose well: Prayer. We are attracted by prayer, and more important still, it attracts God's Love, and jointly we can undertake the work of cleansing, detaching these parts alien to the soul, like the coral which covers the sunken ship.

As an adolescent, I used to retire frequently. In my free moments, I liked to climb atop the hills, to withdraw to the forests, and there, in the soothing atmosphere of nature, enter into conversation with the Heavenly Father. My mother called this "mysticism," this strange communion with nature. Well, in some way this was true, but still more, it was the contact with my Heavenly Father, my conversations with Him, and the immense happiness offered me by this proximity with our Creator, who for me didn't live far away up in His Heavens, but very close, so near in fact, that I could so easily turn to Him in all my concerns and worries.

Conversation, you ask me? Yes, they were really conversations, and they continue this way, even clearer, more transparent and translucent. And as you now *receive impressions, and questions and doubts are forming in your mind, the same happened with me, and the answer arrived immediately, like in your case. Am I not responding to your questions? Aren't you the one who conducts, in some way, this communication, through your questions and doubts? Ah, you're beginning to realize! And you feel very happy; it is one of the happiest moments in your life, and you can repeat it - we can repeat it! We are awaiting your call, but we are also waiting for you to get into the necessary condition so that we can really take advantage of this opportunity.*

My dear brother, we are anxious to get into close contact with you, with all of you. So, give us the opportunity, get ready, tune in, and you will live, even here on earth, in heavenly moments, moments all of you may enjoy, if you only get ready and contribute your share to this mutual enterprise.

Think it over, listen to me, and may God bless you all,

Jesus.

© Copyright is asserted in this message by Geoff Cutler 2013

A sensitivity to the presence of spirits is indeed the first step to communication and increased inner sensitivity is part of the natural outcomes associated with prayer and development as a medium. Traversing that road blindly is not recommended and is the same as taking the journey without a solid grounding in Divine Love. Jesus speaks eloquently on this subject and assures us that our sense that there is indeed communication, no matter how subtle, between spirits and mortals is real and can be a dynamic part of life. Our doubting minds throw a wrench into our efforts to recognize these realities. It was not that long ago that people were put into insane asylums for claiming to 'hear voices', and before that they were burned at the stake. Understandably we shy away from going beyond the common belief that such things are 'in our imaginations' rather than something far more interesting and useful.

It is widely known by those who experience spirit and angelic presence that we all have guardian Angels, and those who are adventurous enough seek to forge a bond of clear communication with them. This may be your motivation or at least may form the beginning of your journey. Rest assured that there is a great wealth of experience waiting for the willing traveler. The key is to put in safeguards and parameters so that you won't fall off a cliff through ignorance or carelessness. Yes, there are some who have been reckless and consequently have found themselves in mental institutions or completely alienated from reality. The purpose of this book, in part, is to guide you safely through the door of an alternate reality that is very real and powerful. The next chapter is about my journey through this door and I want to share it with you so that you might better understand the perspective and knowledge contained in this book.

Chapter 2

Coming into Mediumship, the Author's Story:

I have been a Divine Love medium since 2011. I did not seek out this gift but rather I was asked to accept the role as a medium by my Celestial guides. I have been deeply involved with praying for Divine Love since I was a young man of 20 and as I write this I am now 65. The first gift that I recognized and pursued was a healing gift which I still practice to this day. I did not think of myself as having the gift of trance mediumship as there were those whom I have shared this path with who demonstrated mediumship since the very beginning of my journey. I was glad to sit back and listen as they went into 'condition' or a trance state and verbally channeled many Celestial spirits. This was a comforting and nurturing relationship with my dear friends who willingly brought forth these loving words and impressions given to them by the Angels. This most often happened in a prayer group which I was a part of from the beginning. For many years I was very content and grateful for such an arrangement while in this prayer circle

About ten years ago our beloved friend and channel started to experience health problems which affected her gift to the point that she could not channel in a very effective way this great variety of spirits. Though we continued to pray together in our group setting, receiving the Love of God, this other aspect of our shared experience was greatly diminished because of the medium's failing health. As a medium, she went into a very deep trance and never remembered anything about what transpired through her. Her singular objective has always been to be a channel for the highest spirits, our Angelic teachers and to this day she continues to be close to her beloved guides and teachers. Her example has always inspired me to seek for the highest in any spiritual work that I might pursue and I believe that we were brought together so that I might learn from my beloved friend and mentor how Divine Love mediumship works. It is quite clear that having such close contact with her seemed to have rubbed off in many ways

While my mentor continued to struggle with her role as a medium and generally to navigate through life, I received an unusual request from my guides while I was in meditation and prayer. I clearly remember hearing them say "We wish for you to step forward". My immediate response was a resounding "yes" but I really was not clear about what they were asking of me and replied "and do what?" Again, they asked me the same question and I answered, this time with a bit of exasperation, with the same refrain "and do what?"

I suppose at this point these lovely Angels were reminded that they were dealing with a rather guileless and straight-shooting sort and changed their tactics. "We wish to speak through you" was their direct response and I was a bit gob smacked with this invitation. All I could say in response was the classic "Who me?" As I considered their invitation I felt unworthy and unqualified for the job. Having my wise friend and mentor demonstrating to me all her strong and loving abilities with such dedication and loving kindness for so many years, I felt very small compared to this spiritual giant of a woman. They assured me, however, that I was indeed up for the task and that I had been prepared for it in many ways by them, by my friends and by my own soul growth.

I felt, however, that I could not decline, although I knew that the Angels would never force the issue nor blame me if I refused. Something inside of me knew that this was the right course of action and a true gift even though I never considered it in any serious way before. I said yes, with the caveat that I was to be a channel only for Celestial Angels as my mentor had been and that I would be protected at all times. My guides readily agreed to my terms and so I started this fascinating and very fulfilling journey of trance mediumship. One that I have never regretted taking on.

My first message came through at our regular Monday night prayer circle. I had explained to my fellow sitters, who had been a part of this circle for as long as I, that I was asked to step up as a medium and was willing to try that night. A message did indeed come through and the speaker said that this was not the first time I had been used in this way but the first time I knew that this was the case. My innate faculty to be a medium was there all along, but my mind could not accept this to be true until now.

Since then many Celestial Angels have spoken through me and a few thousand messages have been received. Most of these messages were received in small prayer groups which we call circles of light. Also, some of these messages have come through larger retreat settings and when my wife Jeanne and I are together in prayer. Jeanne always has with her a recording device that catches the message and we are fortunate enough to have several volunteers who transcribe, edit and post them on line.

There are very few who are engaged in the work of being a channel for the Angels because of the time, inclination or know-how required to be successful. By default, I and a few daring souls have engaged in this work. It has always surprised me that this retired landscape gardener is a part of such an unusual endeavor.

The work however is as exciting and meaningful as it is somewhat unique. Though there has been some notoriety in certain circles, I never wanted to be in the limelight. I feel that what has been accomplished to date has little to do with me but much is the result of this dedicated band of Angels who are working through me. Humility is a great asset when pursuing this work. Those who are seeking recognition and even fame need not apply. The Angels do not work in this way. Rather they go quietly and gracefully about their business sowing the seeds of truth and Love. 'There but for the Grace of God go I' is my credo and so far, God has graced me with incredible experiences and opportunities. My hope is that He will continue to guide my path forward and may He bless others who are interested in serving in this way.

I believe that there is no limit to what a gifted group of mediums dedicated to God's Service are capable of. My efforts here to share what I see as the way forward in developing good mediums for the cause of Love and Truth, constitutes my primary motivation in this regard. I think that it is important to formulate and share standards that ensure success and consistency. It requires a firm grounding in the Divine Love truths as part of everyone's journey of service in this capacity. We will try to cover as much ground as possible in this book. Our angel friends have certainly conveyed much wisdom in their messages on this subject so we will rely heavily on their guidance.

Since this book is intended to be a guide and clear road map towards becoming a Divine Love medium capable of communicating with the Celestials, what form that communication might take is partly dependent on soul growth and partly upon the gifts that you may have inherited from your predecessors. Since natural mediumship is often an inherited trait, bringing with it some forms of brain wiring and chemical markers in the body, not all folks can take up the task easily. Mediumship can be developed without such attributes, but possessing them makes the process much easier.

No matter what form this gift might take, there is always an avenue, possibly not as you envision it, but still available to ensure some form of communication is developed. Everyone is different in their abilities and spiritual gifts, so my experience as a trance medium may be quite different from yours. It is in the differences and wide range of the expression of these gifts that many aspects of spiritual truth may be given and valued by those who are on the receiving end of it.

This is not a step by step template that you are obligated to follow. Instead the intention is to help you to mark your own progress on this path and recognize some of the sign posts and pitfalls on the way. Unlike the physical world, the reality of spirit that exists outside these parameters, and also within you, is not predicated upon a rigid set of rules and consistent principles. As with many things in our lives, there are hard and fast principles to follow but the route to understanding and adopting them can be as varied as there are people. Since there are so many subjective perceptions and sensations involved in this process, one cannot make your experiences the standard for another's. That said, there are indeed spiritual laws which need to be understood and acted upon. It is in your personal experience and sensations of opening up as a medium that makes the journey unique and makes you unique in your gifts. This part of the journey is impossible to standardize, but there are many subtle aspects and shared portions of wisdom in the chapters to follow and added messages from the Angels. Hopefully you will gain much confidence as you absorb the wisdom from the Angels and from other's experiences. It is not an easy journey to delve beyond the standard reality of mortals, but I can assure you that it is not dull nor without its rewards.

Chapter 3

Angelic Connections

Celestial Angels are spirits who have received the inflowing of God's Love to such a degree that all traces of the human condition or inner disharmony have been released. Because their souls, minds and hearts are now in powerful alignment with God and His laws of Love, they are fit to reside in the Celestial Kingdom. These are the highest (closest to God) spheres of existence that any spirit can progress to. The Celestial Heavens are apparently limitless and one's capacity to be close to God has no end for a Celestial being.

This is not true for those spirits who have pursued the development and refinement of what we call their 'natural love' capacities. They will end their journey at the sixth sphere of spirit known as the natural heavens. Their souls cannot progress beyond this point because, though their souls have been completely cleansed of error and disharmony within their pursuit of perfection according to the natural laws, without accepting the inflowing through prayer of God's Divine Love, they cannot enter the Spheres of the Celestial Heavens. They have become perfect human beings but not beings who have been transformed by God's Essence into something more than human.

There is certainly progress within this sphere or heaven, as their minds continue to seek further truths, but the light within the soul, as distinct from the mind, can only progress to the point of purification. Without experiencing the transformation of their souls with the 'New Birth', they are limited to the natural heavens

The impetus for those who inhabit the Celestial heavens is to seek at-onement with God. Apparently they continue to progress and are discovering new truths all the time. As mortals, our ability to receive or comprehend what the Angels wish to convey to us in terms of truth is certainly limited by our own soul's growth and mental capacities. Until the faculties of the soul, which is our untapped resource needed to understand truth, is opened with the Divine Love, we are limited by our gifts of mental deduction and our level of soul development. Hence a medium that is able to progress further into soul awareness could conceivably bring through higher truths than what we presently possess on earth. Our goals then, whether we are pursuing the gift of mediumship or not, are to further awaken our souls in the way that has been prescribed. Fortunately, with soul awakening, the gifts of communication through mediumship, clairvoyance, clairaudience, clairvision and other intuitive understandings all come to us in good time as we pursue the gift of Divine Love. Our souls are full of gifts and wonders that most of us are barely cognizant of at this stage of our development.

The following message from Jesus through another Divine Love medium known as D.L. gives us a good insight into the perspective of the angels regarding soul growth and gifts of mediumship.

Automatic Writing and Thought Impression.

Spirit: Jesus, August 31st, 1987

Dearest Master, I have just read and re-read your last three messages through K.S., finding them to be most wonderful and informative. I only hope that your message through me today can be as helpful to humankind.

I would wish that you speak on whatever law or subject you wish to address today, but I do have one question for you relating to how my own particular mediumship works. Mr. Padgett seems to have submitted such control to you that you and others had been able to not only use his brain but also his writing hand to communicate your and others' messages of the past. Now, with me, I am neither aware of being in a trance nor am I conscious of any control being exerted upon my hand when I receive a message from you. I receive thoughts dictation-style, if you will, and I am conscious of my doing my own writing of these thoughts I receive.

In other words, what I write is not "automatic" but purposeful on my part - at least, this is how it seems to me. Can you confirm this or otherwise explain how my own mediumship channeling works? Is it really necessary that you or any spirit control a medium's hand in order to get an accurate message through? Of course, when I say this, I realize that my brain is being controlled or used; otherwise your thoughts would have no medium or channel to make transmission possible. But perhaps in my case it would be more accurate to say I receive your thoughts inspirationally (through impressions upon my brain), but not automatically (in the sense that my hand is being controlled as well).

Thank you for your help with this, Master. I now welcome your loving presence and message of today.

> *I am now here to write, my dear brother in Christ, and again I am most happy to come to you to attempt to assist you in your understanding of both the subject you*

have addressed and other Truths I wish to make known to humankind. I am your friend and brother in spirit, Jesus, Master of the Celestial Heavens and the eternal leader of our church on earth.

As to "automatic" writing channeling and how this works in your own particular case, you are correct in your statement that you receive inspirationally from me and, in turn, that you consciously write the thoughts that I am able to successfully transmit through your brain.

Not all mediums receive in precisely the same way. It is true that the degree of control possible varies from medium to medium and in accordance with the medium's own gifts of reception. What is important is not how completely a spirit controls but how effectively and well a medium receives. And, as you know, this is dependent upon the medium's own soul development and his preparation to receive some of the higher Truths of God.

The Laws of Rapport and Communication have been clearly spelled out by my cohort, John, (This is covered in the next chapter) and need not be repeated here; for you are well familiar with his messages on this subject, and you do know that it is the relationship one has with the Father - the amount of Divine Love received from Him in combination with the medium's own soulful aspirations to know the Truth that determines the level of receptivity of the medium at any given point of time.

It is not necessary for a medium to be able to achieve a deep trance or for a spirit to actually do the active writing of the message that the spirit is transmitting. As I once suggested through K.S., which suggestion started your own apprenticeship in this area, all that was important or necessary in your case was to sit quietly pray for protection and guidance, and then help write the thoughts that would be transmitted by me or others through your brain; and you have done this successfully thus far and it should not be a cause for concern on your part with regard to who is doing the actual writing as long as you fully believe that the thoughts you are recording come from us and are not the product of your own thinking.

You are correct in your understanding that all thoughts coming through one's brain seem to be one's own, whether these be the mortal's own thoughts or the thoughts that a spirit is impressing upon that mortal. But, as you have read and re-read the messages already transmitted through you, already I am sure that you are coming to understand and appreciate more fully that the thoughts you have received have come from a higher source than your own mind.

I do know that you doubt this at times, thinking that perhaps you have lent a bit of your own creativity to these messages. But I can assure you that the thoughts you have received in the very great majority have been our thoughts and not your own. Of course, the language or particular words used are sometimes selected by your own storehouse of words, as contained in the repository of your own brain's learning and storage, but the meaning given to you, which sometimes is translated into words with which you are familiar, comes from us. If you were reporting inaccurately, as in the case with K.S., you would be told, and provision would be made for the particular message of that day to be repeated at a later time when you were in a proper and more receptive condition of soul and mind.

I do not want you to have anxiety about your ability to receive our messages, for you do have this ability and it has been demonstrated amply in the messages already transmitted and recorded. For, as you know, your faith and confidence in your ability to receive well is an important dimension with regard to how well we are able to transmit our own thoughts through you. One can easily set up blocks against receiving well if preoccupied with a shakiness of faith during periods of actual message taking. But I am happy to say that blocks have rarely occurred with you thus far, and I am confident that we will be able to continue to transmit our thoughts through you successfully and accurately. Just keep praying to the Father for improved ability, as you have been, and both your faith and your ability will continue to improve and enlarge.

As to Mr. Padgett's channeling ability, as you have deduced before in your own thinking and analysis upon this subject, he was not entranced when taking our messages; neither was he oblivious to the thoughts coming through his conscious mind at the time he was actually receiving our messages. Had this been the case, he would never have interrupted our communications to have asked questions about the information he was actively receiving. It is true that a certain amount of energy was transmitted to him, along with our thoughts, so as to enable him to persist with the recording of some of our longer communications. However, while it may have seemed to him at times that he was not doing the writing - so intense was his concentration on our thoughts rather than upon his writing of our thoughts at the time - in point of fact, he assisted in the writing of these thoughts, just as one writes one's own thoughts when this is done by the person receiving impressions from his own brain apart from any spirit's impression upon the same. But, as I say, the energy given to Mr. Padgett to receive and write our thoughts did cause him to feel at times that the pen or pencil was writing "on its own."

I hope I have answered your question satisfactorily for now. The important thing is not to understand all the finer nuances of how mediums may differ in their reception of messages, but to concentrate on the development of this God-given talent so as to be able to continue to receive our messages accurately and well for the benefit of humankind. And you have been told that the proper development of this ability continues to depend upon increased receipt of the Father's transforming Love which acts upon both the faith of the medium and upon his increased ability to receive clearly and more easily without any blocks interfering; or perhaps I should say with blocks becoming a greater rarity as this receptive talent enlarges.

I think this is all I wish to say on this subject for now. Owing to the length of my explanation, I will postpone a more formal message to the next time. However, I wish to say in concluding this communication that I am well pleased with both your development and the sincerity of your ongoing efforts to improve your channeling ability. But you must not lose sight of the fact that you have come a long way already in the relatively short time that you have been receiving my messages. And I want to thank you for your devotion and persistence with this task of receiving our messages for the benefit of others. Just keep praying for God's Love and for increased ability in this area, and you can be assured that neither the Father nor we will let you down. The Father knows of your sincerity and desire to improve and ever do well, and He would not have selected you to perform this work if you felt otherwise. So, as I say, have faith and persist and the reward of mediumship excellence will be yours, along with the knowledge that you have been an active contributor for the dissemination of more of the Father's higher Truths to humankind. That blessing alone, as you know, few have been privileged to realize.

So, my dear brother, I will leave you now with my blessings and my love until next time. I am

Your brother and friend, Jesus.

It is easy to recognize the difference in language and approach between the medium known as D.L. and that of H. who has been identified in previous messages. It is important to take note that every medium will receive a message differently than what may come through another medium.

As Jesus indicates in this message, the Celestials are interested in all forms of mediumship for the purpose of communicating higher truths. D.L.'s gifts were not like that of James Padgett's who received his messages through the gift of automatic writing. D.L.'s mediumship came through the infusion of his mind with inspired information which he wrote down as a form of dictation. The accuracy of his writings was verified by Jesus in this message and he is encouraged to continue. Other mediums, such as me, are less conscious of the information being conveyed as the Angels use our brain and voice to communicate. There comes a fleeting knowledge of the words meant to be spoken but that familiar flow of thoughts – which come with normal speech or conversation – are not present. Think of it like the prologue in a Star Wars movie as the words come into focus on the screen. There is certainly a sense of words coming, but they are unclear until almost the last second. This is certainly for me a clear indication and signal that I am indeed in a state of trance and my material, as well as spiritual faculties, are being used to communicate.

 Most developed Divine Love mediums have some awareness of the presence of the Angels during communication. Some see them, most feel their loving presence and depending on the intensity and closeness of the rapport, there is an overwhelming sense of love and joy. Being that close to an Angel brings a sense of pleasure and spiritual upliftment not readily available with many other experiences. Certainly, a deep state of prayer and communing with God can bring further dimensions of awareness and deeper feelings of love and joy, but I have found that as a medium in session with the Angels, this experience comes with less effort and more consistency over time. It is a very welcome byproduct of their presence and I am deeply grateful for the energetic conditions that they bring, not just to me but to all present. God's gifts to us are multidimensional and generous. I always look forward to that boost of light that my Angel friends bring when they come into rapport. Although I clearly understand that without consistent and regular prayer for God's love, such a rapport is not likely. One leads to the other as this is the very foundation of this work.

This message received in a Divine Love circle in Vancouver B.C. almost 60 years ago also encourages the mediums and sitters to forge ahead with their spiritual development and communications with spirit.

Suggesting that a School for Mediums may be established.

Spirit: JAMES (APOSTLE)

> *I also would like to speak a few words to you; I am James. How pleased I am to come and blend with you in love. The harmony which is developing between you and the love which is growing between you I trust will be that which will grow into the force that will give to you the gift of direct voice. A strong love force is needed between us and so many of us work together with you my friends.*
>
> *Solomon is with us tonight and you know that he is a powerful and wonderful spirit and he brings with him great love for this group and he desires very strongly that a foundation should be built where people may come and learn the truths. That the teachers of truth may come and spread to all mankind, God's wonderful*

plan of salvation and the wonderful gifts which God has in store for you. There are so many spirits that desire to help you, desire to come and it is so important that other souls develop spiritual gifts. We need good mediums very much, but mediums must have the foundation of Love within their souls to do the work which is required on this earth plane. It is very important to us to have many mediums in all phases of work and development. But it is so important that the ground work be laid for the progression of these mediums.

I would like to develop here a school, a school for the development of mediums, grounded in the Truths of God, a foundation of God's Love. It is important that these Truths be spread about the Earth quickly and to do this we need those who will work unceasingly and selflessly to serve God. So, we need someone, we need those who can teach in truth, those who are strong and can lead, where new souls can be brought into the fold. They require nurture and love and the strength of those who have been in this work for longer periods of time. For in the beginning their gifts are weak and their soul development lacks the strength. It is important that you have a strong love bond between you, that you have something to give to your weaker brothers and sisters who will be drawn to you and who will be necessary for the work in the years to come. There is so much to be done. We need so many workers.

We need the love force and the harmony that is necessary to develop the spiritual gifts of these new souls who come to you and seek but you yourselves require spiritual food and it is good for you to gather together as a close-knit group in love and harmony where you can feel at one and go forth again into the world. I am pleased to see you draw together as you have tonight with strength, harmony and love which grows between you, for the work which is before you.

We strengthen you in our love and I want you to know too and to feel that God also is in this room with us. We are not separated from the Father and the Love and power of God. Feel that God is in the room, feel the Love and harmony strengthening and growing between us. Continue on and know that you are blessed of God and that your efforts are blessed, that we are with you to support you. My children and my friends, I love you very much, each one of you. I love you so very much.

Celestial Angels can certainly come close to mortals though I suspect that a full-on rapport would be more than any mortal could stand. Yet we are miraculously blessed with their assistance and upliftment. They encourage us to continue to progress and to help others to progress in the 'Love'. They come as a result of our desire for Divine Love and an awareness of their presence is dependent upon our ability to perceive the Angels who accompany this experience.

Our next chapter covers the laws of communication and rapport in order to give clarity to the process. I will conclude this chapter with the following two messages, one given through me and the latter through the medium H. who lives in Ecuador. The first message is a rather long and detailed talk from an ancient guide who lived in Egypt five thousand years ago and is now a Celestial Angel. The second message comes through H. from his guide Judas. It not only provides good advice for mediums but for anyone who desires a close connection with the Angels. Again, you will notice the difference in styles of wording and approach. H. received his messages in Spanish which were then translated into English, so some editing was done in order to make the sentences flow better. I also edit those messages that come through me for grammar and sentence structure before I publish them.

Spirit: Seretta Kem, March 27th, 2016

God bless you, my brothers and sisters, it is your servant and brother Seretta Kem, and I promised you that I would return to reiterate a message regarding mediumship.

So many laws come into play when this gift is used by a mortal: the Law of Attraction, the Law of Activation, and the Laws of Love combined with the desire of the medium and what is their intent, their desire to be used in this way, their minds focused on various subjects and imbued with various bits of knowledge, and with that of course is the development of the soul.

When we angels are able to use a medium, this comes about because that medium has received within their souls a certain measure of Divine Love causing an attraction, an affinity and a certain measure of understanding of these Truths of God's Love. As the Love strikes a soul and imbues within the soul a certain amount of understanding, awareness, capacity and perception to know God, to know His Love, to perceive the angels, opening up this world, the world of the soul, which is not often glimpsed by mortals. The soul is often ignored, buried under many, many layers and mental understandings, beliefs and biases. This is why we encourage you, my brothers and sisters, to go deep within your soul, to establish that connection in a conscious way with your soul. For the truths of the mind are transient and often illusionary, but the truth of the soul is solid and can be relied upon. These truths must travel up into your mind and in this traversing into your mind; it is often filtered and distorted by those conditions within the mind, the material mind.

So, in the case of mediumship, what may begin as a pure understanding within the soul which comes from the rapport between an angel and the mortal along with the mortal's connection with the Heavenly Father, the message will come through to a degree. That passage is narrowed partly by the encrustations of the soul, the mental understandings, the biases, even fears which will limit this flow of information. It is difficult for the mind to put words to something which the soul experiences in a wordless way.

This is our challenge and when we partner up with a medium to bring forth these Truths, which often that medium has a clear understanding of within their soul but does not have this clarity within their minds, there is some distortion. Not so much error, but an incomplete picture, an incomplete flow of information. As that soul grows and the channel becomes clearer and stronger, it is for each one of you to understand the Truth of God and you must enter the passage that flow and connects your mind with your soul and can bring this information, this experience, to a conscious level. This is done through prayer and what you call meditation. It is done through plummeting into your soul, to release those conditions within your mind, to having a trust, a faith and the assurance that what lies beyond your mental imaginations is something greater, fuller, richer and more aligned with Truth, and less aligned with the human condition.

It is the power of God's Love within your souls, my beloveds, that draws you there, pulls you deeper, allows that consciousness to become recognized and understood. When this is accomplished and an Angel is in rapport with a medium or with any of you, certain information and experiences flood your consciousness and you become inspired if you will, you become in tune with what is happening within your soul and the knowledge and truth that God brings into your soul through the inflowing of His Love. This is the Essence of God, and imbued within the Essence of God is the Truth of God's Creation, existence, Laws and many aspects, all aspects of the universe come with this great gift of Love.

In many ways, the understandings of the soul are far greater, richer and deeper with the resources laid up within the soul than of the mind. As the medium progresses, as each soul progresses, this information is released, it drifts into the consciousness of the mortal, until that flood becomes so powerful, so complete that the mind capitulates and allows this greater, deeper consciousness to inhabit all aspects of the mortal. When this is fully embraced, when the soul is cleansed completely from all its sin and error, its encrustations, the mortal becomes redeemed, an angel and at one with God and that resonance and great awakening is complete. Yet it does not end there. Just as God is infinite and immortal, just as the universe is infinite, so the awarenesses, the understandings, the embracing of God in all His great and wondrous power of Love goes on for all eternity. I know this is hard for you to comprehend in this limited plane that you exist upon, but it is so, it is a Truth.

We in the Celestial Kingdom witness this Truth every moment, continuing our journey to God and at-onement. It is our pleasure and gift and blessing to come to you, my beloved brothers and sisters, to encourage you upon that Path. And we make great effort to do so, for this increases our joy, our blessings, to have that opportunity to love a mortal. If you may, think of this as a parent nurturing a young child, the joy that that parent has watching that child grow and mature. This is our joy, to watch your souls blossom in Love, to see them flourish in Light, to see how you enact this change within you and your lives, to help you and inspire you to come to God in prayerful communion. This is our joy and it is our privilege.

When we may teach through a medium, some of these

truths and lessons, though as we have indicated are rather incomplete, yet the essence of what we teach comes through. And for souls so young, these simple Truths are what are important, what must be focused upon and nurtured within you. One step at a time, beloved souls and one Truth at a time, to bring it fully within your consciousness and within your heart so that you may ever step forward and grow in this Love and change your perspectives, perceptions, understandings, knowledge, wisdom. As this shifts gradually towards the Truth more in harmony with God's Laws of creation, His Laws of Love, you increase your Light, you walk that path ever closer to God and upon that path you release your burdens, feel greater joy and harmony within you as those conflicts of yesterday are no longer there today.

So it shall go, unburdening yourselves and finding freedom and joy. As your souls long for this, you feel the longing within you. You desire greater Love and harmony, peace and joy. You reach God, you reach out and God responds and blesses you, blesses all around you. As you come closer, He is able to use you as an agent of His Love, an instrument of His Will, a channel so that He may reach through you to others. When you are able to release your need to be in control of this, you will feel the flow more intensely. It will carry you through your life and you will not be reluctant or ambivalent. You will allow — and joyfully so — God to guide you in your life. You will willingly go for the joy in this, the power of this, because the effects of allowing God to use you as His channel of Love will far outweigh any detriment you may imagine and will heal and put into harmony all aspects of your life in ways that you cannot imagine. God knows what is required, how your path will be traversed, each one unique, each one beautiful and each one purposeful.

So, my friends, you are on a wondrous journey and those

who are gifted with the gift of mediumship are entrusted with a purpose that has a measure of influence upon each of you and allows us to speak more clearly about your journeys, about this Path, the Truth of God's Love.

There are no perfect mediums in this world. Each one influences what is brought through and this I believe we all understand and accept, but it is your love and support both given through this medium and towards the medium, which encourages and sustains and allows us to come through as we do. It is important that you send your love to those who speak. It is important that you encourage those who speak. For it can often be a struggle and there are doubts that arise and I know that many of you benefit from these messages given which helps to clarify your path. There are times when the message given — or portions thereof — do not resonate with your understanding. Have compassion, beloveds, do not reject this, but understand the challenges that are in place for this type of communication.

Yes, you all desire for the highest and so do we. But the highest, my beloveds, is a graduated thing. It is dependent upon the conditions within the circle where the message is received, the aspirations of those within the circle, the condition of the medium, and the aspirations of the medium. There are many elements at play. We must all work together to bring ever higher Truths, clearer Truths that resonate with the soul. We are working diligently to do so with this medium and other mediums in the world. It is your prayers that are important. And there are disciplines that each of you must carry out to ensure that you walk the highest path. It is especially important for the mediums to be disciplined and prayerful and desirous of the highest Truths.

So I have explained a portion of the dynamics and

elements involved with this gift of mediumship. I am pleased to do so and each of you must take into account what has been taught, for each of you is influenced by Spirit, though you may not speak, you are receiving information through your souls and through your minds and these truths and information affect all of you. It is important to understand this.

Many people walk through their lives with no understanding whatsoever of the power and influence of spirit in this world, but it exists nonetheless. All of you, every soul upon this planet, are subject to these influences. It is important to understand that this knowledge arms you so that you may not be subject to negative influences and that you do indeed reach for the highest and attract the angels by your side. We may assist you with every aspect of your lives, bringing our wisdom, bringing the blessings of God's Love, helping you upon your path, praying with you and protecting you.

As I have spoken to you in the beginning about the Laws that are involved in mediumship, they are involved with each soul, the Law of Rapport and Communication, the Law of Attraction, the Laws of God's Love. It is very important to understand, my dear friends, to keep consciously aware of how these laws affect your lives and influence your decisions, and how your decisions influence the effectiveness of these laws upon your lives.

I thank you, my dear brethren, for allowing me to speak this day and I wish you Love. I wish you a great opening within your souls that will revolutionize your thinking and your consciousness, to bring a greater awareness of God into your lives, a greater understanding of what your lives are meant to be, to bring meaning and purpose, fulfillment and joy as God's Love empowers your soul and brings about this great revolution within *you, this cleansing, this redemption, this powerful Touch of Truth and Love. May you all walk your paths with this great power of Love firmly influencing every step as God touches you further upon your path in wondrous ways. God bless you, your servant Seretta Kem loves you and is pleased to assist you. God bless you.*

Trance Mediumship

Spirit: Judas, December 27th, 2001

My dear brother, let's talk about trance. I deem it opportune to address this topic since there have been questions in respect of this. Also, there is much confusion as to the nature of trance and its importance for message transmission.

When you lie down or sit down in a comfortable armchair and relax yourself, imagining how the bed or the armchair bears your weight, feeling some region of your body completely relaxed, and how this muscular relaxation spreads from that point all over your body, when you concentrate on your breathing, when you feel somewhat dizzy and suddenly you feel as if a hand is pressed on your forehead, then you are in trance. Right now, when receiving these words, you are in trance. Your eyes are tearing, but you are not weeping from emotion, it is just one of the signs of trance.

As you see, this is not a very special or mysterious state. You are completely awake, but your awareness is very restricted. You no longer perceive the noise around you, and if I would now prick your skin with a needle, you would feel no pain.

Everybody is able to reach this state. And there are many ways to achieve this. What you are using is a self-hypnosis procedure, a quick and sure procedure.

If you imagine somebody watching a football game on

television, someone who is completely concentrated on what he is observing, and who no longer perceives what is going on around him, you can understand that this person is also in a state of trance. The same thing happens to people absorbed in the reading of a fascinating book, and to the dreamer who later can no longer explain how the hours vanished.

Trance has many faces, from catalepsy to these so daily and common phases. Perhaps this is not how people imagine trance, but it is really.

All those phases have something in common. It is the limitation of perception. Several parts of awareness disappear temporarily; it may be the awareness of what is going on around them, or it may be the awareness of their own body, losing all sensation of pain. It may also be a loss of a yardstick or judgment, and people become very susceptible to suggestions, as in classic hypnosis.

The great advantage of trance for our purposes is that the loss of annoying external influences allows a clearer perception of the spirit's "voice," that is to say, thought impressions, as well as images. Sounds or other kinds of perceptions such as scents or touch are perceived with much more clarity. We could even say that without an appropriate trance state, although it may be very slight, that message transmission is not possible.

From what I have said you may understand that Dr. Samuels also received his messages in a state of trance. However — be careful! — don't make the mistake of equaling trance depth with precision in message transmission.

It is generally believed that when the medium's phrases turn out twisted or incorrect in grammar that means that the medium is in a state of trance and that the rapport with the spirit who is transmitting the message loses strength. I want to remind you that the words that the medium reproduces are not the selfsame words of the spirit. Rather, they have first undergone a process of transformation in the brain, or in the mind, of the receiving medium. Sometimes it happens that the flow of information exceeds the restricted capacity of the medium. In the case of bad rapport, the phrases turn out mutilated, out of context, etc.

I want to remind you of a sentence that was transmitted in a message through James Padgett:

> "This Love comes to men through the workings of the Holy Spirit, causing It to flow into the heart and soul, and filling it so that all sin tends to make them unhappy."

Of course, this is nonsense. The sentence should read:

> "This Love comes to man by the workings of the Holy Spirit, causing this love to flow into the heart and soul, and filling it, so that all sin, which tends to make them unhappy, must be eradicated."

This does not only happen in automatic writing, but also in dictation when deep concentration prevents the medium from realizing the error. Even later revisions don't detect the mistake because everybody knows what the phrase is supposed to mean, and you read what is supposed to be on the paper, and not what really is there. How many people will have read this message without detecting the mistake!

[H: This message is contained in "Angelic Revelations of the Divine Truth," volume II] (Editors note: As also in Vol III of "True Gospel Revealed Anew by Jesus")

As to the observation that the messages received by Dr. Samuels have a strong Jewish coloring, this is true and very natural. A medium's beliefs and convictions always *exercise an influence on the contents and presentation of the received messages. The same thing can be said of Mr. Padgett's messages, whose marked anti-Catholicism reflects the beliefs and convictions of his personality. Much of what is criticized there of Catholicism, can also be criticized of Protestant congregations. In addition, a great emphasis is notable on punishment, a relic of his education, something that does not disappear so easily, since it is anchored deeply in people's personality.*

As to the chosen people, it is true what Saul of the Old Testament states in a message received by Mr. Padgett:

"God is not the God of any race, but He is the God of every individual child who comes to Him in true supplication and prayer, seeking His Love and help in his spiritual nature."

There are many more messages on the topic, all of them indicating that God does not have a chosen people. The "chosen ones" are those who choose to be with God.

Jesus was born a Jew. Nevertheless, I imagine that it was also possible that he could have been born an Indian or in any other country. That was God's decision. All humanity has received on multiple occasions and in many ways the revelations of God. Some people preserved them, although not in their pure form, for example the Jews, in whose Scriptures you may learn much about God's nature. However, much of what they contain is also false, such as the image of the avenging God. In a similar way, other peoples received divine revelations, as in the case of the Bhagavad-Gita of India, which also contains a mixture truth and falsehood. Other peoples did not preserve anything in their traditions.

The concept of a chosen people is completely incompatible with the concept of the individuality of man's relationship to God. Dr. Samuels knew this, and, even so, his unconscious left deep prints in his messages.

[H.: I am seeing Dr. Samuels. Are you projecting this image to me or is he really present?]

I am reproducing his image in your mind, but he is really here, and he wants to speak with you.

[H.: I am really trying, but I cannot grasp anything. It does not come through... I only perceive the word "pressure"... ???]

Don't worry. He will come again. You are still in your development, and there is still much to do for you. There are affinities between spirits and mortals, and your affinity to me is very great. However, it will be very difficult for you to tune in to Dr. Samuels since you are not on the same "wavelength." But you will learn. This is why I am your guide, and not he.

But I want to make it very clear that Dr. Samuels' messages, in general, are first class. Especially when they deal with historical topics, they can be accepted with great confidence. Always remember that an isolated message is never very reliable. It is the body of messages that produces reliability.

The medium's beliefs and convictions may influence that message. They are like filters. Imagine a filter in front of the lens of a camera allowing only the passing of red light. All objects of other colors simply are not perceived. And now, when we want to transmit "objects of red, green, blue and yellow color" to the mind with the prefixed filter, a good part of information gets lost. Moreover, what is worse, the medium sometimes fills in the holes in the information with his own ideas, unconsciously deforming what we really want to say. Therefore, we have to carefully select the receivers of our messages.

Some kinds of information are very difficult to convey,

such as names, dates, places, etc. And in these cases, it is a great help if we can have recourse to what the medium already knows. Trance allows us an easy access to the medium's memory and recollections, where all that information is stored with incredible precision. Unfortunately, there is also the danger that the medium himself accesses incorrect parts of this information and interpolates them into the message unconsciously. However this can be controlled provided the medium has the will and disposition to cooperate and to develop.

In my last message, for example, you were not sure if the year of my birth was the year 2 or 3. You wrote down the correct year, year 2. I advise you that when you are not completely sure, follow your "intuition." Write what you are perceiving, do not simply omit things. If you make a mistake, there will always be the opportunity for corrections.

Previously I have mentioned that trance depth does not guarantee precision in message transmission. This is true. And I will explain this to you using an example.

When the hypnotist commands a hypnotized person to kill someone, they will not obey if in their totally awake state they would not normally do this. Or remember what you read on the experiment where the hypnotist suggests to the hypnotized person that a room is empty, when in fact the room is full of furniture and stuff. Then the hypnotist tells the person to cross the room and the hypnotized person obeys, avoiding all obstacles. When the hypnotist asks why the person did not cross in a straight line but by zigzagging, the hypnotized person will invent a series of excuses, for example that he wanted to look out of the window, that a stain on the floor caught his interest, etc. In spite of the strong external influence on the part of the hypnotist, or on the part of the spirit in the case of message transmission, it is the receiving persons' beliefs and internal perceptions that govern their behavior and resulting action. Therefore, my dear friend, perfect transmission does not exist.

In our case, I recommend that you continue practicing. The method of projecting the image of the spirit and your visualization has contributed much to your progress and your concentration on the contents of what we want to communicate. I am happy with what we have achieved so far. God willing, next year will be a prosperous year in this sense. We have come to the most important part of Jesus' life, and in the first place I want to tell how he taught us his message of God's Love.

Now I will conclude this long message.

My dear D___, I hope I may have provided you with some clues for your undertaking, which we watch with much happiness. Be assured that you have all our backing. I would also like to tell you that you may trust in your perceptions and in your guidance to select the pertinent passages for your book. It is a wise decision to select and rearrange. In order to convey a concept, it is certainly not necessary to reproduce all the messages phrase by phrase, word by word.

But now, I am really through. I say good-bye, with all my love to you.

Your brother in Heaven,

Judas

It is important to note that it is not necessarily the depth or quality of the state of trance the medium is in which determines the quality of the message received, but rather the desire of the medium to give a higher message and whether they are in alignment with the path of Divine Love. Both Seretta Kem and

Judas stress the need for higher aspirations and thoughts as well as having faith that truth will come through with soul aligned with God. With the right set of circumstances and innate abilities, Celestial messages are possible, but there are many things to take into consideration. The next chapter on the laws which need to be observed in order for any communication will help you to understand these requirements.

Chapter 4

Knowing the Laws of Communication and Rapport.

Geoff Cutler on his website, new-birth.net has compiled a comprehensive discussion on this subject using excerpts from the Padgett messages. James Padgett was born on August 25th, 1852 and died on March 17th, 1923. His gift of mediumship through automatic writing was discovered late in his life after the death of his wife Helen, in the year 1914, when he was 62 years of age. The content and wording of these messages is strongly biased by his profession as a lawyer and the culture of his time. Nonetheless, many important and valid truths were conveyed through Padgett and they are as relevant today as they were over one hundred years ago. Padgett was the first Divine Love medium known to us. His work is seminal in understanding the Divine Love Path which leads to the opening of gifts like mediumship. With Geoff Cutler's permission, I have copied the contents of this chapter from his website.

The Laws of Rapport and Communication concern the issues relating to communication with spirit. John the Apostle covers these issues in a number of messages with Geoff Cutler's added commentary.

On January 4th 1918, John the Apostle said:

"As you may know, it has been sometime since I wrote anything of a formal character and I regret very much that so much time has gone by without my being able to communicate some of the spiritual truths, and also regret that your condition has been such that I was unable to make the rapport with you that is necessary in order that I may deliver to you these messages of the nature mentioned. I have explained to you in a former recent letter, in a brief way, the law of communication and rapport, and that law, if you will try to understand it, will enable you to comprehend the reason why we have not been able to communicate these higher truths."

John the Apostle

Here John complains that he has not been able to make a sufficient rapport to communicate higher Truths to James Padgett. He goes on to say:

But, as we have told you before, rapport and our ability to use your brain are governed by laws, and one of these laws is that a high thought cannot be transmitted through a human brain which is not in the condition that qualifies it to receive the thought, just as the brain, in matter pertaining to mere material knowledge cannot receive a conception or comprehension of some intellectual truth with which it has not had acquaintance, and transmit it. A brain cannot be used by the mind of the human to make known or present a problem in geometry, when that brain has never been used by the mind to acquire an acquaintance with or knowledge of the principles of geometry. This is an incomplete analogy but it may serve to illustrate what I mean.

In essence, because Padgett had not spent sufficient time in prayer for Divine Love, or perhaps because he had allowed the worries of his material existence to overly intrude, he was not in a sufficiently good spiritual condition. And, although spirit communication could be made, it would not include higher Truths. This is a law pertaining to the communication of higher Truths. In fact, in the message referred to within the above message as: "in a former recent letter" he goes into more detail.

This was received on November 2nd, 1917:

> *Well, you have not been in that condition of mind that has enabled us to make the necessary rapport with you. We must have a mind that is filled with thoughts of the higher things of truth, even though we do not use those thoughts. Our thoughts are all spiritual, and our truths can be received only by the mind in a spiritual condition, and you, lately, have not had so much of this spiritual mind as formerly.*
>
> *Our contact has not been so close, and our rapport, necessary to enable us to express through your mind these spiritual truths, has not been so perfect. And when I say mind I merely mean the organs of the brain as influenced by the thoughts of the mind; for I will tell you what you may not know, that these component organs of the brain are not always and under all conditions receptive of the same control by the minds of spirits. You may receive through your brain a long and profound message of things pertaining to what you may call the material, and yet under similar conditions of these organs, not be able to receive messages of the higher truths; and the conditions of these brain organs are caused by the condition of the soul in the possession of things spiritual.*
>
> *It is difficult for me to express just what I intend to convey but this you will understand, that upon the development and possession by the soul of things spiritual, depends the capacity of the human brain to receive the various kinds of messages. A medium who is*

merely intellectual and morally good cannot receive those messages of the highest truths, because there can be no rapport between the brain of such a medium and the mind of the higher spirit who may desire to communicate. And thus you will understand why it is that the messages from the earth-bound spirits or from those who have merely the intellectual development, are so vastly more frequently received by mediums than messages from spirits of the soul development.

John the Apostle

In fact John goes on to say that one can search through the history of spirit communication, and not find messages similar to those delivered through Padgett. So, this Law of Rapport which enables Higher Truths to be communicated is extremely important.

It seems that if the mortal exercises his mind in a highly spiritual way, his brain is altered in some subtle way. This allows advanced spirits to communicate at the more advanced level. Interestingly this brain condition is not permanent, but needs to be kept in tune, as it were. Or perhaps it is just as the spiritual thoughts alter the brain, returning to lesser thoughts may return the brain to its former condition. He goes on to extend this idea to the ability of the mind to possess thoughts which it cannot express to the brain. That is precisely the parallel to the advanced spirit having spiritual thoughts it cannot express.

However, this does not apply to purely intellectual truths, and a spirit can take complete control of a human brain, and communicate things, or even languages the mortal has no concept of. As is said here:

But this law, applying to and controlling the relationship of the mind and brain possessed by the same man, does not so absolutely apply to and control the relationship of mind and brain, where the mind is that of a spirit and the brain that of a mortal, for in such case the mind may take such complete control of the brain, that the former's manifestations are not governed or limited by the special experiences or want of experiences which the brain may have had in its use by the mind of the mortal along specific lines of expression or manifestation. Thus, as you may know and as it has been demonstrated by the work and experience of many human mediums, the minds of spirits have controlled the brains of these mediums, so that such brains have transmitted from these spirits expressions of various kinds of languages and mathematical truths with which such brains never have had any acquaintance or become exercised in expressing.

In these instances the brain is used merely in the sphere of intellect and the spirit who takes possession of that brain and uses it to express and make known the knowledge of the spirit's mind, is doing no different thing in essentials, to what the human mind, controlling its own brain, could have done had the brain been exercised in those directions. The capacity of the brain, whether exercised or not by the human mind controlling its own brain, limits the power of the spirit to control in the manner and for the purpose mentioned. But this law has a further phase, and that is, the greater the general experience of the brain in its exercise by the human mind, the more perfectly can the spirit mind control it. All this is dependent upon facts which I cannot linger here to explain, such as the mediumistic qualities and susceptibilities of the human whose brain is attempted to be controlled by the spirit.

But while the sphere of intellect may be easy to circumvent, in the sphere of the moral and in the sphere of the spiritual, things are different. This has presented problems in transmitting higher spiritual truths to the world.

John says on January 4th, 1918:

> *You may search the whole history of spirit communications and of mediumship and you will not find any messages of the character of those that have been transmitted through you, and for the reasons that I have stated. Swedenborg was the last and nearer perfect instrument for receiving these higher truths, and yet he, because of his want of soul development and his being bound, to a more or less extent, by his orthodox beliefs and scientific knowledge that caused him to coordinate and fit in these truths with his ideas of correspondence and such like conceptions, was a failure, and could not be successfully used to transmit these truths which we have been communicating through you.*
>
> *And after him other gifted and, in some respects, successful mediums were used by spirits, of the higher knowledge and progression to convey truths, but their conditions were such that, under the workings of the laws governing rapport, these mediums could receive only those truths which their conditions of development permitted them to receive. The workings of this limitation were not dependent upon the condition and ability of the spirits to impart these higher truths, but upon the capacity of the mediums to receive them.*
>
> *You, yourself, have had experience as to how this law works and controls communication and rapport, for, as you know, it has been a long time since you were able to receive any spirit messages of these higher truths, although the spirits have been present with you many times, ready and anxious to make the rapport and deliver their messages; and you have been willing, intellectually, to receive them, but because of your*

condition or want of condition, the spirits could not deliver them and were compelled to wait until you get into the necessary condition. From all this you will comprehend why so very few messages containing high spiritual truths, or even moral truths, come through mediums.

John the Apostle

So we see that in order to communicate higher truths, the mortal must spend a lot of time with his/her mind turned to things spiritual. It is unfortunate that this subtle but critical issue is not more widely known.

One of the things that are particularly interesting is that one can discover that Padgett came in and out of condition. One might think that once in condition, the brain would be ready to receive higher truths from then on. But that is not the case. In fact in yet another message through John, received October 22nd, 1918, he notes that Padgett has still not understood the import of the two messages referred to previously:

I have explained to you the law controlling rapport and communication, and endeavored to make it as plain and understandable as possible, so that you, at least, might grasp its meaning; but, I see there are some things that you do not understand, and because thereof, you have had the recent experience of not being able to receive the many messages that were waiting to be delivered through your brain and hand.

As I have said, the first and important requirement is that you be in that condition of soul which will, because of its qualities, enable the spirits who may desire to write the higher messages to form a rapport or union with you, which means simply to take charge and control of your brain — a brain which because of certain qualities and thoughts having possessed it, will be in harmony with the thoughts that these spirits desire to transmit through it, just as it is absolutely necessary that the medium through which it is desired that the electric fluid shall flow, must be a medium possessing such nature and qualities as will permit the fluid to flow through it. A wire or medium may be made of wood and the electric fluid be present, ready to flow through it, but cannot. And why? Not because the wire or wood may not be perfect in itself as such wire; but, because the wire has not that nature and quality that will permit the electric fluid to make a union with it and thus control it.

And so it is with the brain of the mortal, that such brain has the possibility of possessing, when properly prepared, those qualities that will admit of this union and control, while the wood has not. But the brain, when devoid of this preparation, is just as non-receptive to the union with and control of these spirits — as is the rapport — as is the wooden wire to the union with the electric fluid. You have been told on numerous occasions that you were not in condition and that the spirits could not make the rapport, and that you must make the effort to get in condition; and this assertion and advice are all true. You were told to pray more to the Father and think of spiritual things, and then you would become in that condition. This is true, and the advice is helpful. But you were not told what this praying to the Father or thinking of spiritual thoughts means, and, hence, you may do these things in a way and yet not get in the condition.

John the Apostle

This is quite late on in Padgett's history, and after he had delivered a significant number of higher messages. Sadly, he never did regain the same degree of rapport. While a few "higher" messages follow this date, eventually Jesus stopped delivering messages. John goes on:

He concludes by telling us once again that in order to deliver "lesser" messages, no special soul condition is required. Dr Dave Lampron received a message from Jesus concerning this Law, on June 25th, 1987:

> Now, as to Laws of Rapport and Communication, yes, indeed, these play a most important part in terms of the limit or limits of spirit influence. As you know, there is a Law of Attraction where like is attracted to like, and this law is most fixed or specific in the spirit world and somewhat less in operation on earth. On earth, one cannot always easily choose his associations; he must live with and among those of varying soul conditions.
>
> But on the spirit side of life, as you have been told, the exact condition of the soul determines the exact locality of the spirit. Now, with regard to spirit influence, those of evil disposition do attempt to influence mortals. But it must be kept in mind that they are essentially attracted to those mortals who they feel some affinity with. And mortals, in turn, by their own thoughts and feelings, add to this attraction. You have heard, for example, that when a mortal activates his animal or lower desires, at the same time, he attracts many spirits who have or have had similar desires as mortals, and who still retain these desires as spirits, whether or not these desires can still be exercised in the same manner as was exercised while they were still mortals. And, so, when given the opportunity by the "calling" of mortals seeking such indulgences, these spirits of similar inclination attempt to participate in these indulgences, even if only vicariously.
>
> And, of course, knowing of the mortal's similar desire, every attempt is made to intensify this desire in the mortal to persist in the indulgent activity so that both spirit and mortal can exercise and attempt to fulfill their appetites for these things jointly. Earth life is the great

period of probation. And, indeed, it can be a period of great temptation or a period of relative freedom from corruptive influences from the spirit side of life. It all depends upon the mortal who must come to recognize that he does not live to himself alone, but is ever exposed to both spirit and mortal influence until such time that his advancement carries him beyond the evil influence exposures encountered on lower planes of existence. But if and when desired, during these formative stages of living and soul progression, the mortal recognizes and knows of the help he may ever receive from the Father and His angels through sincere prayer, and he exercises his desire for assistance and protection in this manner, then he will indeed receive this assistance, protection, and freedom from evil spirit influences through the intervention of those good spirits charged with that mortal's care.

Jesus of Nazareth

This is interesting, because here we see that the Law of Attraction brings spirits and mortals into proximity, and then the Law of Rapport and Communication may allow those spirits to impress thoughts into the minds of mortals. If indeed these mortals were more aware of this, they would recognize that they have a spirit associate, albeit one possibly attracted for no good end, if they are not of good spiritual condition.

So, with this comprehensive description of the laws regarding communication it is clear that one cannot just assume that a desire to be used as a medium for higher spiritual truths is automatically granted. As previously stated, our thoughts and intentions play a key role in what we attract and what we are able to communicate through us as mediums. Most importantly however is the condition and longings of our soul towards God and receiving the gift of Divine Love. The foundation built through prayer and soul growth opens the door of Divine Love mediumship and many other forms of communication with the Angels. Communicating with spirits of lower planes does not require this element and because of this there is a great deal of confusion regarding spirit communication. Seeking for the highest is different and the laws function accordingly.

Geoff Cutler, www.new-birth.net

Chapter 5

Phases of Divine Love Mediumship Development

Since the creation of the modern science of spiritualism in the 1800's, much is known about mediumship, though few in our culture know it well. Its practice goes back for many thousands of years. Oracles, soothsayers, shamans and prophets have all demonstrated at least a rudimentary gift for mediumship. In fact, much of our cultural and religious beliefs have been, in part, the result of information from spirits passed on to mortals whether consciously received or not. Of course, this cannot be proven very readily, but people on earth are more influenced by spirits than we are aware and mediumship is merely an overt example of it.

With this understanding, the contention that every thought and idea comes solely from our own mind is contradicted by the experience of the medium and it can be demonstrated that many of our thoughts are not entirely our own. Anyone who possesses some psychic ability realizes that thoughts are indeed 'in the air' and with some sensitivity we are able to capture them within our own consciousness. The cartoon image of a light bulb blazing over the head of someone pondering a question or problem while instantly coming up with a solution is not far off. Indeed, many solutions to all kinds of problems, including scientific ones, can come from outside of us. This message received by the Vancouver Divine Love group several decades ago from Albert Einstein is quite instructive regarding how he came to solve some complex physics problems and how he now continues with his work in spirit.

SPIRIT: Albert Einstein

I will not be able to stay with you too long, my friends, but I have waited so long to join with you and speak with you that I must take this opportunity when it is given to me. As you know, when I lived on Earth, I devoted my time to scientific research that was very successful in some of my experiments thanks, as I know now, to many who are in spirit who were inspiring me. I found that I gained great knowledge when confused or what seemed a blank wall in my research by sitting quietly and slowly picking up as I know now was knowledge given to me by those in higher spheres of life.

I also know that there is not near the power in the atom as there is in the mind and man soon will have greater knowledge of the power of mind. The force that is around one is far greater than man on Earth realizes it is today and when man will train his mind to reach out and feel and be more aware of the force and power that is around him, then he will naturally reach further and study the laws of God. We have passed now the age of ruling by brutal force. We are entering a time on Earth when man is reaching for greater knowledge; the law of force and is gradually beginning to realize the greatest force is the force of love.

The love of God is the greatest force there is and when man on Earth with his everyday life is loving, feels love and wants to apply this love to someone he loves, then there is great force and when man feels this force of love stir within his soul he cannot help but to feel kindly and want to give and help others. If to love one person makes men feel so good and happy within himself and strong and forceful but kindly in using this force, think how marvelous it would be if man would extend his feeling of love to ten or a hundred or to all mankind, what a wonderful life man could lead on Earth.

And now the men of science are beginning to realize on Earth what a force and power there is in men's mind. When man's mind reaches for the love of God which is the greatest love of all and when men apply this love to everyday living as he must do when he progresses in God's Love, then the force will be so strong around your earth plane, that the force of the Love of God which brings that peace and happiness will come to all mankind on Earth.

Slowly those who search on Earth the secrets of science, the scientific laws slowly they realize, that the greatest scientific discovery of all is applying the Love of God in your everyday life. Remember this my friends.

There is no greater force than the mind of man and when the mind of man is governed by the law of God. When man's mind demands the love or the force of God, then all problems on Earth are solved. The law of ruling by force, brutal force, is past and slowly man is seeking to rule by love. Good night and God bless you my friends.

Most of us have no idea of the scope and extent of spirit influence in our lives but even the great Albert Einstein, after passing into the realms of spirit, came to realize that he needed help to bring to fruition his contributions to science. The idea that we are being influenced by spirits may scare those individuals who have a firm belief that the boundary of thought remains within the mind and goes no further than what we decide to share. Emotions are not considered in quite the same way. It is not so difficult to pick up on another's emotional state if they are not overly guarded. If we consider emotions and thoughts as mere energies expressed in different ways, as I'm sure Einstein would agree, then it makes sense that they are not completely contained within the individual but are part of the free flow of energy that is all around us but is often not consciously recognized. We mostly go about our day blind, deaf and dumb to these realities, but ignorance of the law of communication and rapport does not mean that we are immune from its effects. We are not only influenced by the energy signatures of each other but from that of spirits as well. Being armed with this knowledge helps us to navigate our world, not only from that state governed by the five senses but with that 'other' very real universe of thought condition and spirit influence as well.

Much has been written about the state of our world and the earthly conditions which our angel friends describe as dark and heavy. The following message delivered by Augustine, who is a part of our group's band of teachers, talks about the difficulty in knowing the Will of God because the spiritual condition of the earth makes it challenging to say the least. Since the focus of a soul immersed in Divine Love is to know God and His will, this message is not only relevant to those who wish to be a channel for the Angels to speak, it is relevant to everyone who desires to pursue at-onement with God.

The Will of God

Spirit: Augustine, December 12th, 2016

> It is Augustine your Teacher and I wish to discuss the topic of the will of God – how it is manifest in your lives and in this world.
>
> Think of the will of God as a light emanating from the sun. This light is pure, direct and powerful and it has many attributes. The will of God is like this; it shines

forth from God into the entire universe and is unimpeded within the conditions of God's Creation in their pure form. When the will of God comes to this world, however, it is obscured by the clouds of the human condition. That sunlight is diffused and not direct, but at times there are clearings and the direct light strikes your being and creates inspiration, even revelation within you as your souls are quite able to receive this beautiful inspiration from God, His Will resonating within you and then that clear sky often is covered again by the human condition and the light becomes diffused once more.

As these conditions roll in, you also become somewhat confused, your thinking diffused and so the will of God is not as bright, clear and powerful within you. Whatever God has guided you to do, it often gets distorted by your mind as you think and review this gift of inspiration. So you go about your daily life in an effort to apply what is given in guidance. At times this does not seem satisfactory to you because of this weakness in the illumination of understanding.

So you must return to your Heavenly Father in prayer, ask again for His guidance and ask for confirmation of this guidance. Bring your focus back to what has been asked of you and the angels will help to bring you clarity.

In an ideal world, a world clear of these conditions, the will of God given to the soul, enlivened with the Father's Love, would be clear as day. There would be no question; there would be only a joyful enactment of whatever is given in guidance and direction.

You, my beloveds, often have a difficult time discerning the will of God, to collect those diffused rays of light within you, and to make sense of it. There are some more attuned than others who are able to discern more readily these bits of guidance but most of you struggle, you have within you certain ideas and perspectives. You filter the information, make it anew at times, make it into something else that is not relevant to the flow of God's Will and so it goes in your life. You feel you are being tested when the understanding is unclear and you act upon it and find results that are not satisfactory. At times you feel guilty or inadequate or that you have been abandoned by God. This is not so. You are guilty of nothing other than trying. The results may not be as you expect, but there are results nonetheless and God never abandons you.

You are to move forward with the grounded viewpoint that not all of God's Will can be enacted in this world in a pure and powerful way. But there are times when this can be so and the flow of His Will has direct and wondrous results. In these times, you should celebrate that the clouds were indeed lifted and the light did indeed shine and you were blessed and those around you were blessed with whatever God intended for you to be blessed with and that whatever action happened in the world brought light.

You must understand this, my beloveds, that God's Will cannot always be enacted in the world in a pure and unadulterated way. No, my beloveds, but as you grow in the Love, as your souls expand in the Love, it acts to clear away these conditions and brings you into greater alignment with His Will. You begin to have the faculties that enable you to hear and see and understand in a clear way what that will is.

Even then, my beloveds, you still must deal with the human condition in this world and this is a challenge also. Two challenges, one in the clearing of the conditions within your own souls and then the clearing of the conditions around you. As you continue to work in these areas, as you continue to pray for more of God's Love, as you learn discernment, as you grow, as you move in this world and become wise and your perceptions of the soul deepen. You begin to release those deep conditions which distort your thinking and your faith grows and God's Will becomes apparent and a powerful aspect of your lives. You will begin to release the burdens that many of you carry, a sense of responsibility, of upholding this truth in the world and often you feel anguished when others turn away and do not understand and you feel guilty that you have missed opportunities and you do not feel as if you have done enough.

Beloved souls, it is in the growing of your souls that all of these dilemmas will fall away and find solutions and come into clarity. You are not alone, you are never alone and God is joyed by your efforts to be His channels of love and to be close to him. Do not ever feel that you are inadequate, that you do not give enough.

There are always times to pray, my beloveds. If you feel you are at loose ends, pray. If you feel you need to do something more, pray. Dedicate your soul to the inflowing of His Love, for herein lies the key to all. There is nothing to be concerned about other than concern about the relationship between you and your Heavenly Father. In this, clarity will come, the light will shine, the guidance will be given and you will know the joy of that intimate and caring, deep and vital relationship that comes with the Father's Love and His presence within your life, and within your consciousness. It must be a constant shining light for each of you, my beloveds. Allow this beautiful expression to infuse and grasp and envelop every aspect of who you are and every aspect of your life for God's Will to shine through with great clarity and impact, to bring light and harmony.

You continue to struggle, you continue to grow, you continue to pray and this is good, this is the way it must be. And yes, so much of what you have benefitted from; the blessings that are given, the growth that you have made is hard won in this difficult world. You have grown stronger with each day, with each prayer, each struggle, each triumph and you will continue to do so until your days are full of light and clarity, until you are rightfully within the flow of God's Love. This is coming.

You continue to wade into that deep stream. It is coming. Have faith, my beloveds, know that God's Love and His Will will triumph over all and bring to you what your souls truly desire, which is service and at-onement, love and joy, wisdom and peace. It grows within you and will come to fruition in your lifetime.

Blessed are you, my beloveds, for you carry the flame of truth, you are committed, you are growing in strength and always continue, continue to seek His Will.

Your teacher Augustine is always by your side, encouraging and teaching as are many angels who love and support you. You are never alone, beloveds, and we will never leave you.

God bless you, God bless you. I love you.

Augustine certainly assures us that the day will come when clarity of the soul is more predominant in the world. With such clarity, a medium will have far less trouble bringing through a message intended by a Celestial spirit or ideally, we may all have the ability to communicate with spirit directly. He also talks about our propensity to influence and distort things with our minds. With the ongoing development and strengthening of our souls, this becomes less of an issue.

Mediums are gifted with a finer attunement to the thought influence of spirits and the higher the attunement, the higher the level of transmission of spiritual information as mentioned in a previous message from Jesus on page 3. This truth is one of the fundamental building blocks necessary for Divine Love mediumship. Without greater sensitivity and awareness of spirits, we are groping in the dark and are likely to fall into some pretty difficult, if not very unpleasant, situations.

The most common and obvious consequence of developing mediumship is the experience of increased sensitivity. Our emotions are closer to the surface and feelings seem to spring up from nowhere. For years, I experienced severe embarrassment because my emotions would get the better of me. In movie theaters I would weep at the corniest and blatantly manipulative emotional ploy in the movie plot. Yet, I do not seem to have much control over the intensity of my feelings both of joy and sadness. They seem to spring from the reservoir of my soul and as I became more developed as a medium, the floodgates of both tears and joy flow freely.

This is not to say that my emotional life is out of control, but I am often surprised when something deeply moving touches me so profoundly. As a man who grew up in the 50's, such displays of emotion were frowned upon and feelings of shame continue to cling to my mind from these long past programs. The up side is that I am able to feel more readily the intensity of God's Love while in prayer. The down side is that if I see an animal die in a movie, I'm affected sometimes for days. Ironically, I've become so immune to shoot'em up movies that I am as cold hearted as some of the characters portrayed. I puzzle at my own lack of empathy in this regard. The mind certainly does work differently than the soul and both are often a mystery.

Knowledge is certainly power and soul awareness is the most effective way to being attuned to what is around you at any given time. Being aware of these 'other dimensions' of reality requires one to use all of one's faculties without the material mind rejecting or highly censoring the information. Faith in your own abilities to perceive something out of the ordinary is important and having confidence that this is possible requires more than just belief. It requires the knowing of the soul proclaiming the truth of the matter.

Soul faculties are different from mental faculties. The mind receives, categorizes and files information and it is also colored by emotional responses. Our daily perception of reality is built on this process, yet soul perception is a completely different ball game. The soul perceives in a different way than does the mind. It has the capacity to go beyond the mind to a place of what can only be described as multi-dimensional awareness. If we say that the mind is confined to a two-dimensional reality, then the soul is not so constricted and sees reality from what we may consider to be a three-dimensional sphere of awareness. The soul can delve into a number of dimensions of perception and 'knowings' simultaneously.

 In communication with God through prayer, there can be multiple downloads of information that are not just restricted to verbal/ mental input but will utilize other aspects of both spiritual and physical faculties that includes sight, sound, energetic signals and a sort of mindful knowing that can only be from the soul. All mystics know and experience such a state and as one's soul opens to the higher blessings of Divine Essence and inspiration, we can experience it as well. The challenge is to convert such experiences to something the mind can understand and assimilate. This is not easy because the mind is limited by its paradigm of reality and processing capacities, yet when one comes back down to a more earthly reality after experiencing soul awarenesses, there is the memory of the experience and, with time, an assimilation of what has happened. Using two-dimensional communication to explain multi-dimensional reality is similar to the limitations that Angels have when communicating with us. Thus, the extent of what can come through our minds is an ongoing challenge for our Celestial friends. If you have experienced soul perception for yourself then you can appreciate the limitations of the written word. It is safe to say that soul perception is indeed superior to that of the mind when it comes to spiritual matters and it is the faculties of the soul enlivened by God's Love that make Divine Love mediumship what it is.

Intentions play a significant role in spirit communication. Intentions can originate from both parts of us, mind and soul and the key is to harmonize and become aware of what it is that we desire. Since both expressions of intention can be out of sync and possibly diametrically opposed to one another, bringing to consciousness in thought and prayer our intentions regarding the utilization of our gifts is necessary.

As stated previously, the law of attraction brings to us like spirits and if we are intent on the highest of spirits, we will indeed bring them close. I rarely have Angels speak through me without expressing a prayer beforehand. I always pray for the blessing of the Divine Love within my soul and pray for the cloak of protection from all spirits and influences that are not Celestial. Covering these bases may sound like rote prayer but bringing such intentions forward before engaging in spirit communication ensures a measure of protection and a focus on my basic intentions.

Prayer always must be sincere and though I have been praying in this way for most of my life, I can slip into repeating the words without focusing on my soul's longings. This will probably be a lifelong challenge, but I believe that I reach the mark more times than not. The Angels guard me well and I sometimes take their protection for granted, but if my heart is in the right place, it is safe to assume this protection exists.

Success with Divine Love mediumship is not easy if we are out of alignment with the highest. Pretense has no place in the process and discipline in both prayer and thought is a daily requirement. Our prayer life adds another important element to our foundation. Without having a soul grounded in the truths of Divine Love and having received enough of it so that it is a living part of us, there can be no true and reliable Angelic communication.

The spirit Seretta Kem in his last message points out that the material mind must be aware of the Divine Love truths beforehand if one is to be an effective channel for Celestial communication. It is not advisable to put the cart before the horse when it comes to developing this gift. As I have said repeatedly, one must be submerged in all truth and understanding of Divine Love in order to successfully engage in this form of service. My mediumship did not come until thirty-five years after committing myself to this prayer practice. It could be that I'm a slow learner and that my intentions did not lean toward mediumship, but in retrospect I am glad that this gift did not come too soon in my life.

As a retired man who has had a career, raised children and lived a full life, my present, much quieter life has afforded me the luxury of much more time to devote to spiritual endeavors. It is absolutely necessary for one to work towards a condition of light, having our thoughts focused on the highest and a soul focused on God in order to be an effective medium. This is why few of us ever enter into this contract, because it takes a substantial amount of one's time and energies in order to fulfill this role and to serve without a plethora of life's distractions getting in the way. This form of mediumship becomes a way of life rather than a hobby or a curiosity.

Others may not be so involved when their focus is on communicating with spirits in the spirit spheres, but if one is to follow in the tradition of Padgett and other serious Divine Love mediums, then it can only be possible if there is serious commitment. Commitment and mindful considerations must be a part of one's practice and daily routines.

Judas advises H here about the process of becoming a medium. He shares a great deal of wisdom in this message:

Communication & Mediumship

Spirit: Judas, August 20th, 2001

> I am here, Judas.
>
> H.: It is surprising. After our meeting this afternoon, I did not think that we could meet again tonight.
>
> Nothing surprising in that. I told you that I am always with you. And this means that we can always be in direct contact. It only depends on you. Just call me, and I'll be there. Now you can even visualize me, and this allows you to have a little bit more confidence.
>
> H.: Yes, confidence is the most difficult part. I feel so much insecurity, and I ask myself if my mind is not playing tricks right now. I am scared, I don't want to commit errors, I don't want to deceive anybody, including myself.
>
> You need time. Not everything can be developed to perfection overnight. But these are no illusions. You have problems, because my thoughts look the same as your own, that is, you cannot distinguish them. But we are talking, and this you realize. Another problem is that you do not know how to control your mind. Your thoughts come like a torrent, everything at once, all unordered. We can deal with subjects, discuss your questions, but you need to learn to formulate everything clearly, and

then we will proceed to treat your questions one by one.

H.: Supposedly we are talking soul to soul, so I've been told. But what has this to do with my mind?

The impressions arriving at your soul, you transform them automatically in thoughts, into your thoughts. I told you that the moment when the soul takes control is when the spirit is ready to enter the seventh sphere. You are still fixed on your material mind; you still have to go a long, long way.

H.: And in this translation, in this formulation into words, there lies the danger of errors sneaking in?

Exactly. It is then when your own thoughts mix with mine. And it can even happen that you don't translate my thoughts at all, and the output is what you want to come out. You have to practice. This communication is not perfect, but it is the only one we have at our disposition.

H.: Did Padgett find the same problems?

Don't think of Padgett now, or of the other mediums. All men are different, all their perceptions are different, and the mediumship of each medium is different. You are a unique case, as everyone else is a unique case. Don't think of this right now.

We will spend happy moments together. You will go through wonderful experiences, seeing things you have never seen before.

H.: Are you telling me that I will leave my body and travel in the spirit, as it were, like an astral voyage?

No, not at all. But what I see, I can project onto your mind, so that you may see it, too. The sharpness of your vision will depend on our rapport, on your condition. Look right now, you are totally tense, your body is all cramped. You relaxed in order to establish rapport with me, and now after a few moments you are all tense. This is not good, so relax.

Now it is better. And now you are thinking of a specific question, and we will deal with it. Harvin asked about his daughter, who never was born. You know that there are a few messages on the subject. Show them to him. But in order to give him an immediate answer right now, I want you to tell him the following:

Babies who die before being born or a few days after their birth are received by special spirits, who take care of their formation. They are good spirits, and many times succeed to start those babies along the Divine Path.

He also asked if he could see her one day. This depends on the link of love between the parents and their baby. Many parents simply forget, others try to displace the recollection from their memory, because it is a sad recollection, and they don't want it to interfere with their lives. This is very understandable from a psychological point of view, but in all these cases, the love link does not exist anymore, and the spirits in charge of the babies' education and care do not try to establish it. If it does not exist, no artificial link will be created. On the other hand, if there is a loving connection, those spirits stimulate the baby's participation, in some way, in their parent's life. This means the babies spend much time with their parents, they are well informed about their doings and their life, and one day when the parents themselves pass over, the "babies", who normally are not babies any more, receive them and prepare a wonderful welcome to the spirit world for them.

The rupture of family links is not tragic. You have heard that in the spirit world those links will be kept up during some period of time, but then, little by little, they disappear. They are replaced by another form of nexus, determined by the Law of Attraction. The biological family loses its significance. Lastly, we are all brothers and sisters, and material biology, as you know it on earth, has no utility here.

Yes, he also said that the baby still had no name. But tell him that here even the names lose their importance. Names in this form do not exist anymore.

H.: I don't understand this well. How do you identify persons without names?

Someday I will explain it to you. But now, this is not the moment to do so.

You have to work on your mediumship. You must pray. I know, you do pray, but you must pray more, and with more I'm referring to intensity. You have achieved already something very important: a certain opening up of your soul. We can meet easily. But depth is lacking. If you wish profound information, you must have the corresponding disposition.

H.: Will I receive formal messages?

You've already received two. Besides, what is a formal message? We are chatting, and despite the little formality of our encounter, you have already received a lot of information.

H.: But there is something more I do not understand. How do those babies look like who die? I mean their spirit body. Babies on earth grow; develop, through the food they receive, the body shapes in some way until the child has become an adult. Afterwards, there continues a gradual process of decay. But the spirit body....

The spirit body is the expression of the soul. In some way, it betrays the soul's condition.

It is not hard to imagine that the soul of a baby has not much development, and that it practically lacks any *experience, both positive and negative, of earth life, and this experience always leaves characteristic footprints. But it is a pure soul. Hence, also the spirit body is bright, but shows clearly its "immaturity", that is, its lack of development and experience.*

As the soul progresses in its formation, this progress is reflected in the spirit body's appearance. In some way, these babies enjoy a big advantage, because they have the opportunity to return to the spirit world in their pristine form. But, on the other hand, their lack of earthly experience is a disadvantage.

H.: They have advantage and disadvantage, after all, it is just...

Don't talk about just or unjust. We live in a world where justice finds no room, it is a world of love, either the love of man, or the Divine Love, but love and justice have nothing in common. Justice is a human invention. God is not justice, He is Love. If you don't understand this, you cannot comprehend God.

Give me a hug; I have to say good-bye now. We have shared much today. Each day has its task, and we must not overdo it.

Good night, and may God bless you,

Your brother,

Judas.

© Copyright is asserted in this message by Geoff Cutler 2013

The first message that I received from a Celestial spirit exclaimed clearly that 'we only take those who are strong'. As a young man this message was very pertinent indeed. What man in his twenties lives a pure and wholly spiritual life? Certainly not me at the time. Yet, this statement is relevant to any of us who want to serve as a Divine Love medium. Judas suggests to H that he needs to pray more. Padgett received that advice almost daily from his guides and the job of the Angels is to inspire, cajole, advise and lead us to prayer.

With prayer comes the awakening of our potentials and can neutralize our barriers to success. It is in the going beyond the superficial that accompanies so many of us through life that a spiritual perspective is gained. Prayer, prayer and more prayer is the key to opening up our higher potentials. In awakening the soul by receiving the Divine Love, we will find our way home. God grants us many gifts, much of them dormant in our souls. How else do we come to understand the language of the soul unless we go to prayer and open up the reality of God's Universe? With this, the practice of mediumship is just one aspect of our soul's awakening. Having a consistent and focused prayer practice on Divine Love adds another piece to the foundation of the development of mediumship.

Elevating our thoughts along with a commitment to a regular prayer practice and a focus on receiving communication from the highest source leads to the awakening of the soul. With this comes humility and patience, faith in the will of God and trust in the process of soul awakening. All these elements contribute to the foundational development of Divine Love mediumship. It Is a tall order for any of us to commit to such a venture given the many demands and distractions in our lives, but it is not impossible. Motivation is a key, as is discipline.

Those who are too eager to seek a message from spirit without applying the slow and steady regiment which has been suggested will undoubtedly receive some form of communication. The question is 'is it of the highest'? There are signals and routines that can be developed to assure the medium that indeed a Celestial is communicating. In our next chapter we will explore this important subject now that the ground rules have been established.

Chapter 6

Knowing the Spirits

Within the Divine Love Community there is a great deal of interest in mediumship. Since this form of communication has played a major role in the investigation of the truths of Divine Love, many of us continue to study spirit communication and especially communication with the Celestial Angels. The words given to us by Angels such as Jesus and his disciples through James Padgett and others, often opens the door of our mind and soul's understanding of what true spiritual awakening is. It captivates and excites the imagination of the seeker who may have started with traditional religious thinking but has sought to go further. In comparison, what is imbedded in these communications completely shatters much of traditional Christian thinking; even Eastern thought is challenged by these communications since the concept of reincarnation is refuted.

These truths are about the development of the soul while humanity has spent a great deal of effort on the intellectual understanding of spiritual matters rather than going straight to the awakening of the soul. This is not unheard of in the world, but certainly it is not commonly practiced either. Those who do focus on the soul are often encumbered by mindful notions that obstruct, rather than open, the awareness of their own souls. Though Jesus taught this way while on earth, his teachings have become so distorted that recognizing the simple practice of receiving the Divine Love is not readily revealed in places like the Bible. Often the revelations received through Divine Love mediums are both inspiring and challenging, but with such insights we begin a journey towards coming closer to God and our own souls.

A common question is "why do we receive primarily messages from individuals who are well known in the world"? There are many examples of spirits who have communicated but are not famous, yet the majority of the teachers who come through Divine Love mediums such as Padgett and others are those who have made their mark in history. Of course, we all are curious about such persons of distinction, although I don't believe that this is the primary reason why they come. My understanding is that their communications lend credibility and authority to the message more than an unknown individual would. They were very exceptional and gifted souls while on earth and there is no reason why they would not continue in their development and gifts both in mind and soul as they continue to progress in the world of spirit. This makes them very good candidates for further sharing of truth with mortals.

A very important truth is demonstrated in this way. All of humanity and all of creation, for that matter, is in a constant state of change. Nothing stays in stasis but continues to be in flux. Therefore, evolution continues for eternity and our individual destinies are to grow, expand and become perfected within our true essence in our lives here and in spirit. Although perfection is not necessarily the goal, it is paramount that harmony is. The surest way to foster harmony comes with the expansion of our souls receiving the added energy of God's Divine Love. There are those from long ago who have discovered this truth and put it into practice. These beautiful souls who have been transformed by God's Love and are now angels, are eager and willing to assist us in our soul growth.

Being human, we tend to listen to someone who we respect and admire rather than a person we have no knowledge of. Jesus and his disciples are leaders and very high teachers. We are privileged and blessed to be able to communicate with them as we do. They are also very motivated to bring truth to humanity. Thus, we benefit by this mutually attractive situation as the angels are drawn to assist us and we are open to their ministrations. It is the power of Divine Love that makes the connection possible as the laws of attraction and activation are enacted.

In exploring these truths of Divine Love, we might be drawn to the idea of becoming a medium like James Padgett. All things spiritual become a fascination to us and it is natural that many of us might want to experience communication with the angels first hand. James Padgett is likely put upon a pedestal and seen as a role model since his gifts brought to us such rich rewards. Becoming a medium is often glorified and revered as a coveted gift as it may be a chance for us to be a part of something greater than ourselves. Like romantic love, we fantasize and exaggerate the ideals of mediumship and want a piece of it in some way.

While some consider Divine Love mediums as 'chosen' others have little faith that what is received is reliable. There are many pitfalls however, since communicating with Celestials is challenging for both the receiver and the sender. It is important to realize that the predominant energetic conditions of our earth plane are not spiritually advanced or even in the light, so the possibilities of direct connection and accurate communication are anything but easy. It is very clear that motivation, intention and soul development are necessary for success.

No one else has received such profound messages regarding Divine Love both in scope and breath than did James Padgett. The four volumes of work published and which contain his messages are essential reading for those who have committed themselves to living the Divine Love Path. There are those, however, who do not condone others engaging in the development of their gifts as a Divine Love medium. These naysayers may have a point in as much as what is contained in Padgett's volumes has more than enough information to guide one on this path and that there is no need for duplication.

Unfortunately, the language and style of writing of Padgett's era has a certain formality and cultural bias that discourages modern readers. Despite the treasures of spiritual teachings contained in these volumes, many find them unreadable. Padgett's work does not jive with modern preferences in language and political correctness. Instead, it seems to epitomize those challenging forms of communication long lost to history. Yet, if one is patient and able to forgive the cultural norms of the day, there is a wealth of information contained within his writings. The dilemma of those eager to share this information with others is that although the truth written in Padgett has been available in publications and many forms of social media, the growth of this knowledge amongst the many spiritual seekers of the world is pitifully slow and infinitely small compared to the billions of souls on our planet.

The Padgett volumes are not hitting its mark in any appreciable way and this begs the question of how to make the truths of Divine Love better known. Hence developing more mediums with contemporary values and communication styles is one possibility that some have come to see as a solution. The pitfalls of such a venture are many and the commitment involved by those who are both gifted and eager is highly demanding as we have already discussed. To engage in a project of this order, making close rapport and communication with these spirits who live far and beyond the earth plane, requires multiple steps of development and a careful, incremental plan of execution.

The difference between expressing the gifts of mediumship made famous by the Long Island Medium on television and what we are discussing here is very far apart indeed. Celestial Angels are more spiritually advanced than those spirits who are apt to communicate through the majority of spiritualists today. To be effective as a Divine Love medium, one needs to be dedicated not only to the path of receiving and growing one's soul in Divine Love but to working towards and sustaining a level of spiritual maturity and focus which brings a consistent rapport with our Celestial teachers. Our audience is very different, as proof of life after death is already a given for those who take the Divine Path seriously. Those who read Divine Love messages are usually looking for further instruction, assurance and inspiration on how to sustain the journey of our soul's awakening through Divine Love. Certainly, we are all curious to hear from relatives and famous people who have passed on but our focus for the communications feeds our soul's longings for spiritual progression rather than yet more facts filling our mind's hunger for intellectual truth.

Becoming a medium does not mean that we lose all sense of self and give over to the will of spirits. This is often the fear of newly emerging mediums. It was certainly my fear as I began to open up to this gift. My concern centered on the prospect of sounding like an idiot while channeling a message or possibly bringing something erroneous through. Still to this day I have some concerns about these issues. So far, my fears have not been founded other than the odd slip of grammar and pronunciation. These things are readily fixed in the transcription phase so that I am rendered a proficient communicator.

I owe much gratitude to my band of angels who look after me. My 'gatekeeper' especially is an important member of that team since he is charged with keeping out unwanted spirits.

The angels will often use a more colloquial style and sentence structure, not because they are casual in their speech but because I am and they must navigate the thought and speech patterns of my brain in order to bring their communications to physical form. Since the level of trance that I experience is quite light and I am well aware of what is going on, I believe that my mind has a greater influence on the words used by the spirit communicator. Other mediums that go very deep into trance have no recollection whatsoever of what was said through them. I am not of that ilk; rather I am happy to have some measure of awareness and involvement in the process. This is not to say that I orchestrate what is going on, rather I move a step back and allow the spirit to step forward. This is the job of any medium and the more that they can detach from the proceedings, the better the channel.

In order to be used as a medium, certain brain functions play their part in relaying information from the mind of the spirit to your conscious self, triggering words and thoughts that are not your own. The frontal lobes of the brain play their part but not as a primary element in communication. Much deeper and older parts of the brain are more engaged than our reasoning functions. If a brain scan was taken of a medium conveying a message from spirit, many parts of the brain would be lit up on this scan. The Limbic system is deeply engaged as is the Cerebellum, temporal lobe and the speech centers. Often the medium feels that they are in a sort of semi-awake state. This is because much of the higher functions are less engaged and the emotional/feeling centers are more active. The functioning of the brain in the case of mediumship is not well understood as science grapples with giving any credibility to it. Brain science is more focused on practical research and trying to solve serious diseases of the brain than this esoteric practice. Maybe sometime in the future more research will help to clarify how these faculties work together to create the proper conditions for successful communication. Until then, our reasoning minds will have to trust that the certain internal mechanisms work together to bring forth a message from spirit.

As I have said, when a spirit desires to speak through me, I am quite conscious of the fact. This is because I have a band of angels who work with me so that proper communication takes place. Every Divine Love medium is assigned at least one gatekeeper. Their function is like that of a traffic controller who acts like the secretary of a CEO who must approve access to the boss. They perform a valuable function in as much as the medium is often not clear as to who it is that wants access. Thus, they guard the medium from unwanted spirits. Most often, I am aware of my guide Andrew when a message is to come through, although I don't believe that he is my gatekeeper.

I believe that the angel who plays that role does not want me distracted by their presence and goes about their task quietly. Angels are, if anything, humble and uninterested in recognition. They serve God and recognition from the Divine Source is enough. I don't know who my gatekeeper is but I am certainly happy that someone has my back. Andrew's familiar presence both reassures me and gives me a sense of settling into the flow as I get ready to give up my conscious control of the situation. Other signals often precede the spirit's communications as well. In every case, I must feel the presence of the light and love that the angels carry. Without this unmistakable aura that accompanies all Celestial angels, I exercise my right to refuse the rapport. There is a sense of upliftment and a Godly presence when this connection is made. Often, I feel their love for me and sometimes sense what it is that they wish to communicate.

When the higher angels, such as Jesus, Confucius and Augustine come close, there is an atmosphere of power accompanying their love energy and their spiritual presence is often unmistakable. Jesus brings such a sense of love, peace and humility that one is apt to tear up and feel humble as well.

The most powerful spiritual upliftment and conditions capable of bringing the Celestial angels in close rapport to a medium are often realized in a group setting. A group of like-minded individuals praying for the inflow of Divine Love and who project love and good intentions towards each other is the ideal atmosphere for communication. In this climate, the medium is upheld and those around him or her who are giving their love to the instrument are performing an important task. Since a 'circle of light', as we call it, is essentially a container for energy flow and transmission, each participant has their role to play as a 'battery' or reinforcing link in the circuit of energy created with their mutual prayers and loving intentions. If all is in sync and harmony, a message of very high caliber can be obtained along with the benefits of receiving other blessings. Group prayer then is an important catalyst in both receiving a message and supporting a medium in their development and work.

Being blessed with a high Celestial presence is certainly the icing on the cake in the practice of mediumship. How many get to have such a close rapport with the Master of the Celestial Heavens? And such a connection is not easily obtained or common, though some claim that it is for them. Jesus is very busy in his work for the kingdom and to assume that he has all the time in the world to be in close and frequent rapport with you is unrealistic. He certainly can come close and I have known his presence many times, but I certainly do not consider him as one of my familiar and usual band of angels who work with me. His presence is a welcome gift and often unexpected, but to expect daily rapport with the Master is not likely. Many claim that this is so, but in my experience, Jesus comes when there is something important to say or a significant blessing to be bestowed upon us. Otherwise, he leaves the day to day spiritual ministrations to others who are all too happy to serve.

We all have guides and gatekeepers. They perform their roles beautifully and often quietly as these beautiful angels are a great boon to us mortals. Everything functions within God's Economy and wisdom. It is better that we are satisfied and grateful for the many blessings bestowed on us, including those beautiful angels that assist us on every level, than to have unreasonable expectations because we may naively think that such things as having Jesus as a guide is possible or even likely.

As long as I receive my familiar signals from spirit, I am comfortable enough to allow their rapport with me. This is a very intimate connection as another soul comes very close, probably closer than many mortals have experienced in relationship with another person. The keen perception of an angel gives them an insight into us that is greater in depth than we have of ourselves. Everything is revealed in one glance to an angel. Yet they do not judge us but rather have a deep love for us. If you believe that you have any secrets that an angel may not know, then I suggest that you do not have a clear understanding of the power of their soul perceptions. It is nothing like what our minds perceive. The dimensions of knowing through the soul are beyond explanation. What little experience that I have had in this arena has given me a glimpse as to the capacities of the soul to know things that are certainly unknowable by mere mortals and in this experience, one is humbled by what we are incapable of perceiving through our limited material minds compared to our developing souls.

A well-developed soul can see anything it wishes of another soul and if you are shy about being honest and open with an angel, you are not being realistic as to the depth of an angel's knowing of your true self. It is easier to just assume that they know everything about you and accept this as the first step in making contact. Their love for you is undeniable and unconditional. It is closer to God's Love than any other source other than God Himself. Given this reality, fear of an angel is not reasonable. Rather, expect that your life will be an open book and with this in mind, we need to keep our thoughts in check and positive.

Any action that we willingly take has its consequences and negative, unloving acts can damage our rapport with the angels. Taking on the role as a medium for the angels has its responsibilities. Fooling yourself, or ignoring what you instinctively know is a negative thought or action will not ensure consistent association with the angels. They are remarkably tolerant, as they too have lived on the earth plane and have had to expiate their own dark conditions and soul encrustations. Overt and malicious acts of an unloving nature will do little to ensure that the angels can make a close rapport however. The spiritual laws ensure this to be the case. Much to our benefit, they make a great deal of effort to stay in connection with us. There are precious few mortals who are capable of a conscious rapport with the Celestials, so each soul who at least tries to do so is given quite a lot of leeway. This is certainly not a free pass, but it often brings into our lives a special dispensation in this regard. I call this "God's Credit Card." It can be interpreted as an investment in you that God and the angels make, hoping that it will pay off in the future. Considering how far the Celestials must come down to our vibration in order to make rapport with us lowly mortals, certain extra blessings and dispensations must be given in order to excite our interest and facilitate a close rapport. The efforts that they make on our behalf is beyond our understanding and perception. It is truly remarkable what lengths they go to in order to establish contact.

My initial experiences with the angels years ago were quite dramatic and extraordinary. These prolific encounters have not been repeated to any consistent degree, but this was enough to seal the deal for me in my commitment to the way of Divine Love. I have certainly benefitted by God's merciful and generous nature and the angels convey these blessings in many ways. Since so few of us who are willing souls exist in our world, we are tenderly uplifted into conditions truly beyond our normal reach. This helps us to forge a consistent relationship with our guides and teachers. Their efforts to uphold us are great indeed compared to our rather paltry prayers and actions which often lead us down dark paths. Never underestimate the power of God's Blessings along with His angels to assist you upon your journey towards light. It is truly a remarkable gift of love and compassion that reflects the nature of the Divine Love.

Chapter 7

Limitations and Possibilities of Divine Love Mediumship

Spirit communication of any sort is fraught with inconsistencies, misinterpretations and the infusion of ideas and biases of the medium. A good medium can be defined as one which has an adequate level of knowledge relating to the information that a particular spirit wishes to convey as well as a tendency to try not to interfere or edit the words spoken through them. Our minds can be rather sly and manipulative when it comes to spirit communication. Often, we are completely unaware of its interference when channeling a message and the ingrained thoughts that are within the material mind have their influence as to what can be said by the spirit. This is true for any sort of mediumship and anyone who has taken some form of mediumship training and development has been taught to be aware of this interference from our own thoughts. Unfortunately, there are no perfect mediums in this regard. We all bring to the table a complex set of beliefs, experiences and biases which will affect the content of the message given by any spirit using a medium. With this limitation there is also the added requirement for a soul to be awakened in Divine Love to some degree in order to channel Celestials. It is a fine balancing act for any spirit to communicate their intentions and words with some accuracy. For Celestials, their task is indeed daunting, as they must use instruments on earth who are emerging into the light rather than redeemed within their souls by God's Love.

Whether it is a platform medium giving a message of reassurance to a concerned loved one grieving a mate who has passed into spirit or a Celestial angel who wishes to bring through a high spiritual teaching, the challenges have some similarities. The basic mechanics of communication are the same, but the motivation and focus of the medium can be as different as night and day. A strong rapport must be established and adequately maintained if a spirit is to communicate properly. It is doubly difficult for Celestial spirits to maintain a rapport with mortals as the conditions are so different between the two places. Only the power of the Divine Love in the soul of a mortal makes such a venture feasible.

Since we are all human, our personal negative thoughts, feelings and judgments can influence the outcome and content of what is meant to be conveyed. Such energetic conditions may severely affect the message to the point of completely distorting the intentions of an angel's message. This is why so much advice is given for ensuring a high standard regarding a medium's spiritual condition are in this book. Yet there are many things in life that can blindside and throw a medium off their game.

Inconsistencies from day to day are the norm rather than the exception.

I've known a number of contemporary Divine Love mediums, in fact I would say that I have met all of them with the exception of H, and they have all, without exception, had their highs and lows in this regard. Most of them have not been able to sustain a consistent rapport with the angels for one reason or another. It is difficult to maintain a life that is free of distractions, medical impediments and life restrictions which can severely affect this work.

It is also important to note that it can be very difficult for a Divine Love medium to also work with spirits in the lower planes. Maintaining rapport with dark spirits, no matter the good intention to help them, can weaken and eventually break the rapport with the angels. It is believed that James Padgett lost his rapport with the high spirits for just this reason. He found more purpose and interest in helping his friends and other spirits in the earthbound planes than his work to bring further truth to humanity. His example is worth noting as an important lesson for aspiring Divine Love mediums.

Personally, I suffered a mild stroke about a year ago and found that the quality of the messages given through me were much less impactful during my recovery period. Thankfully, my health and vigor has returned to normal without any permanent damage to speak of. One never knows what the future will bring and only the commitment of a number of serious Divine Love mediums will ensure a constant and reliable flow of communication with the angels .

The following message given by Judas through H addressing a number of issues regarding consistent channeling of Angels reveals many impediments to the process.

Channeling and the influence of ingrained beliefs.

Spirit: Judas, January 9th, 2002

> *H.: Dear Judas, I would like to know a little more about soul perceptions. I still have a very blurred concept in that respect. For example, in my conversations with M___, she claimed that the inner voice is not the only form of soul perception. I suppose that this is correct.*
>
> *Judas: Yes, this is correct.*
>
> *H.: Then, when we discussed the subject, I wrote her:*
>
> *"Yes, there are more perceptions [...]. What we hear, apart from our inner voice, what we "feel", when somebody behind us stares at us... Well, we perceive the concentration of other people on us. We don't feel "the pressure of their look," but their thoughts. Not in the sense that we read their thoughts, but rather, we feel emotions, intentions, something like that... This is called empathy, I think."*
>
> *And she responded:*
>
> *"Perceptions of others, of their thoughts and feelings and intentions!! H___, this resembles what Jesus calls communication from soul to soul. This is*

extraordinary. It is necessary to pray sufficiently, H___. Although lately I have wondered, what does it mean to pray, because I am reciting silly sentences? Or, at least, so they seem to be. What does prayer mean?"

And here, I have two questions. Firstly, whether it is correct what we concluded, and secondly, really, what does prayer mean?

Let us first deal with the second question. Since you have been interested so much in the teachings of Lacan, in the registers of the mortal's reality, the Real, the Imaginary and the Symbolic, I will use these terms.

God belongs to the Real, or rather, He is Reality. You can only approach Him through the Real, and not through words, which belong to the Symbolic. The world of God is not the world of language. To recite automatic prayers is like reciting the multiplication table. You have already read this. Words only are effective when they are accompanied by what comes from inside, from the soul, because the soul also belongs to the Real. It is the image of God, even if it is not His Substance. God communicates from soul to soul. Man can also do so, but in the world of his reality, the world that he perceives as reality, he does not in general do so.

Prayer does not need words. It needs desires, longings, it needs heart. We could say that prayer is the intent of coming closer to God, of approaching at-onement with Him. It is our small step to bridge the distance between Him and us. We take one step, and God covers the rest of the way, He comes closer to meet us. He gives us answers. And His answers are not words either. Because His answers also belong to the Real.

H.: I think I can understand this.

Then you understand that it is possible to be in constant prayer, without pronouncing a single word.

But now to the other question. Yes, the sensation that somebody is staring at you is a form of communication from soul to soul. You do not perceive words, but you perceive information loaded with positive or negative values. You perceive feelings, intentions, and attitudes.

In message transmission, the following happens: You know already that the soul can emit and receive signals. And, as a matter of fact, it does so constantly. However, when we are able to concentrate on the signals we are emitting, and when a mortal tunes in to that signal, we speak of the formation of a channel. It is the principle of "channeling." If the mortal is not tuned in, but we concentrate our signal on him, he also receives the message, but without much clarity. He perceives impulses, desires, etc., and so in this way we can try to exercise our influence on people, although they are not tuned in to us.

The soul's "radar" antenna always covers certain areas. And when this area is our frequency band, we will be very successful, and negative influences will pass by without effect on the mortal's soul. When the area covered by the radar is the negative sector, the influences of negative spirits will manifest themselves in the form of desires and impulses within the mortal. Do you understand this? OK.

H.: And Divine Love has to do with transmission quality, I suppose.

Right.

H.: Does Divine Love work then like optical fibers in comparison with a conventional copper wire?

Judas (laughing): We are already sounding like a telecommunications manual, but yes, the comparison is useful.

When one of the parties in the information transfer does not have optical fibers, the signal will come through distortedly. This is why it is so necessary that the medium always prays for more Divine Love. Besides the obvious benefit for the mortal, it also improves communication with us.

H.: How is it possible then that mediums without Divine Love communicate with spirits lacking the Love of God, and that the results of these communications seem quite satisfactory?

We now find something the psychologists call "the lying mind." The information arrives blurred, not very clear, but the medium's mind fills in the holes with their own ideas. They add adornments, etc. This happens when the received information is contrary to the beliefs of the medium or incomprehensible to them.

H.: Then, in these cases it is not a communication from soul to soul? In one of your messages you told me so.

This is correct. They are thoughts of the mind that

come from this kind of spirit. But, as in the example of prayer, these thoughts bear a certain influence from the soul. In the case of negative spirits, the negativity of their bad intentions arrives in the mortal's soul in form of desires or impulses. This happens when the mortal is tuned in some way to the spirit. I have already said that each soul has the capacity to filter certain frequencies. But in many cases, they don't do so. They are like ships adrift, lost in an ocean of influences, accepting anything that may come.

But I want you to explain in detail, for those who may read this message, the "lying mind."

H.: You have in mind the experiment of Freud?

Judas: Yes.

H.: Freud hypnotized a person, in a room full of furniture, and he suggested to him that the room was completely empty. Then he ordered him to cross the room, heading for the opposite wall. The person obeyed, avoiding all obstacles. When Freud asked, why he had not crossed the room in a straight line, the hypnotized man invented a series of false excuses. He said that he had seen a stain on the floor that seemed very interesting to him, that he wanted to look out of the window, and many other things, in order to justify his behavior. That is to say, even in the presence of reality, his mental condition didn't admit it, and in order to justify his behavior, he lied.

Judas: Very well, this is what also happens in message transmission. I want to review with you now a few messages that James Padgett received in the beginning of his career as a medium.

In one of the first messages, his wife Helen conveyed to him the following:

> *"The savior of men. He was with you and I was so glad as I feel that you will now believe that I am in the spirit world and in the Love of God. He is the Lord who came down from Heaven to save men."*

Pay attention to "He is the Lord who came down from Heaven." It sounds like the creed Padgett professed. Padgett, unconsciously, interpolated something that seemed correct to him. "The Lord" in a religious context is always the synonym for God. However, this is certainly not what Helen transmitted to him.

In another message, very soon afterwards, Jesus said:

> *"I came to tell you that you are very near the Kingdom, only believe and pray to the Father and you will soon know the truth, and the truth will make you free. You were hard hearted and sinful, but now that you are seeking the light I will come to you and help you, only believe and you will soon see the truth of my teachings. Go not in the way of the wicked for their end is punishment and long suffering. Let your love for God and your fellow man increase."*

Just look, "their end is punishment and long suffering." This is one of the basic doctrines of orthodoxy. Punishment for the wicked ones. But in later messages, Jesus explains that God does not punish.

In the same tone, Helen wrote:

> *"Yes, and I have seen the spirit of Rector, he is not the spirit that he represents himself to be, he is a wicked spirit who goes about to deceive the mortals on earth, he is a wicked spirit who has no love for God or man, and he is trying; to lead mankind to believe that he is the Christ, he will be severely punished at the time of reckoning."*

Pay attention to "he will be severely punished at the time of reckoning." Once again, the idea of punishment, and additionally, the idea of the "time of reckoning", that is to say, the Day of Judgment. A concept that later on would change dramatically.

Padgett, still without major (soul) preparation, asked Jesus: what does it mean to be "born again?" Jesus answered:

> *"It is the flowing of the Holy Spirit into the soul of a man and the disappearing of all that tended to keep it in a condition of sin and error."*

Once again, an idea that later on would change. Padgett, at that moment, did not grasp it. He had no idea of what is the Holy Ghost, and confused It with Divine Love.

Soon after, he had already grasped the concept:

> *"Do not be discouraged or cast down for*

the Holy Spirit will soon fill your heart with the Love of the Father..."

And also the idea of punishment for the evil-doers began to change in **shades of meaning**:

"The Love of God is reaching out for every man so that the meanest will be the object of His care."

But at the end of the same message, he **relapses one more time** into his ingrained way of thinking:

"The world needs a new awakening, and the infidelity and unbelief of men who think themselves wise but who are foolish, as they will ultimately find out, and the material things must not fill their souls much longer or they will suffer more than they can imagine."

Apart from the distortion in style, this sentence no longer transmits love but threats.

If you study James Padgett' messages in chronological order, you will realize how Jesus, step by step, was preparing James Padgett. This not only used to happen during the séances for message receiving, but all the time. Jesus dedicated a lot of energy to influence Padgett.

The first steps were the most difficult. Jesus did not begin at point zero, that is to say, with a blank and unbiased medium. He had to eradicate deeply ingrained beliefs, and that took time. Eventually, the messages improved notably. Padgett was an extraordinary medium, and of good will. And only being so was it possible to achieve this.

Later on, when there were already people who knew the basic concepts of the Gospel of Divine Love, it was much easier to give new shades and colors to the rough and rigid lines of the original messages. Jesus' message does not change, because it is also part of the Real, but the perception of men changes, and their capacity to understand and to incorporate additional tonalities.

Don't worry, I have not forgotten about the message or rather messages on faith. But today I have overloaded you. We have touched your limits, and I should not proceed longer. You did not grasp everything; it is only the skeleton of what I wanted to communicate, lacking all the meat, leaving more questions than answered doubts. However, I am content.

I'll see you soon again. So long,

Your brother in the spirit,

Judas.

This message from Judas has certainly given us many things to think about in regards to our development as Divine Love mediums. It is interesting that even Padgett, who was the most competent Divine Love medium ever to have channeled these truths, took some time to hone his skills and flush out a number of erroneous beliefs. That is how we all proceed in the development of this gift. It is a constant state of improvement and gaining soul understanding that will ensure that we are an effective medium.

Many are reluctant to take on the task because they do not want to be saddled with the responsibility that comes with it. No one wants to be the one who brings forth error in the name of truth. Yet, to some degree we will indeed do so. Unfortunately, it is our fears combined with our egocentric mind which does the most damage in the beginning of mediumship development. We often seek perfection and are reluctant to proceed unless we feel that we have gotten it right. Yet developing as a medium can only be an incremental and a somewhat experimental process. It requires us to learn how to tone down the inclinations of the mind in favor of the wisdom of the soul. Going too quickly for the golden ring can propel us towards disaster as much as resisting a slow and steady flow of development. The sweet spot lies in daily prayer, faith in the timing of the emergence of these gifts which the Angels are in charge of, and having the humility to love ourselves and see through our headstrong desires to be without fault in our pursuit of perfection. God's intentions for us is to always seek harmony. With harmony our needs are met and everything unfolds with grace and joy.

Mediumship has many different forms and as stated, no two mediums are alike. This brings a texture and style to the information conveyed with each message given through different mediums. The same basic information intended by the Angels can take a variety of forms, approaches and syntax. Judas through H gives us some good examples of it in this message:

Truth and False Beliefs - Part 3.

Spirit: Judas, May 17th, 2002

> *Now, dear brothers, I intend to deliver one last message to conclude the small series on the spreading of Truth, and on the obstacles that are present in this aspiration.*
>
> *I would like to ask you, who does spread the Truth? You? We? The answer is simple: we do it jointly. We try to communicate Truths in small portions, so that you can digest them, and you should assist in their diffusion on earth. Not only the so-called "mediums" who receive this information, but also all who desire to receive it.*
>
> *Now, there is a "Divine Love Movement," and in this group people collaborate who strive for attaining the New Birth in their souls and the transformation of their natural souls into divine souls. But there are also many more people in the most diverse churches that unconsciously aspire to the same objective. I say unconsciously, because they lack the basic information in their minds. However, in their souls, there are the same longings as there are in yours, and this is why they also receive the Father's answer, in the form of the Holy Spirit that conveys His Love into the souls of all His children who ask for It.*
>
> *The information that we transmit becomes words in the mortal's mind. It is an automatic and at times very painful process for us, when the mortal's conception translates our message in a way that makes its results almost unrecognizable. Then, you*

wonder, why do we communicate with people that lack the necessary preparation to guarantee a "trustworthy translation" of what we impart? And my answer is that our message is always very simple, and the essence of what we want to communicate, indeed escapes the deformation through the human mind.

And now, to illustrate just what I have just said, I want you to paste the latest messages received in Medjugorje.

Message of April 25th, 2002

Dear children! Rejoice with me in this time of spring when all nature is awakening and your hearts long for change. Open yourselves, little children, and pray. Do not forget that I am with you and I desire to take you all to my Son that He may give you the gift of sincere love towards God and everything that is from Him. Open yourselves to prayer and seek a conversion of your hearts from God; everything else He sees and provides. Thank you for having responded to my call.

Very well. Now I will write down a possible version, if you or any other Divine Love medium had received this message:

Dear brothers and sisters! Rejoice with me in this time of spring when all nature is awakening and your hearts long for change. Open yourselves, brothers and sisters, and pray. Do not forget that I am with you and I desire to take you all to the Love of God that He may give you the gift of sincere love towards God and everything that is from Him. Open yourselves to prayer and ask God for the New Birth of your hearts; everything else He sees and provides. Thank you for having responded to my call.

Message of March 25ᵗʰ, 2002

Dear children! Today I call you to unite with Jesus in prayer. Open your heart to Him and give Him everything that is in it: joys, sorrows and illnesses. May this be a time of grace for you. Pray, little children, and may every moment belong to Jesus. I am with you and I intercede for you. Thank you for having responded to my call.

How would this one look like if written by a Divine Love medium's pen?

Dear brothers and sisters! Today I call you to seek at-onement with God in prayer. Open your heart to Him and give Him everything that is in it: joys, sorrows and illnesses. May this be a time of grace for you. Pray, my brothers and sisters, and may every moment belong to God. I am with you in order to give you guidance. Thank you for having responded to my call.

The apparition:

Dear Children! As a mother I implore you, open your heart and offer it to me, and fear nothing. I will be with you and will teach you how to put Jesus in the first place. I will teach you to love Him and to belong to Him completely. Comprehend, dear children that without my Son there is no salvation. You should become aware that He is your beginning and your end. Only with this awareness can you be happy and merit eternal life. As your mother I desire this for you. Thank you for having responded to my call.

Now, the other version:

Dear Children! As a mother I implore you, open your heart and offer it to God, and fear nothing. I will be your guide and will teach you how to put God in the first place. I will teach you to love Him and to belong to Him completely. Comprehend, dear children that without the Father's Love there is no salvation. You should become aware that He is your beginning and your end. Only with this awareness can you be happy and inherit eternal life. As your mother I desire this for you. Thank you for having responded to my call.

Message of February 25th, 2002

Dear children! In this time of grace, I call you to become friends of Jesus. Pray for peace in your hearts and work for your personal conversion. Little children, only in this way will you be able to become witnesses of peace and of the love of Jesus in the world. Open yourselves to prayer so that prayer becomes a need for you. Be converted, little children, and work so that as many souls as possible may come to know Jesus and His love. I am close to you and I bless you all. Thank you for having responded to my call.

And here comes our version:

Dear brothers and sisters! In this time of grace, I call you to become friends of Jesus. Pray for peace in your hearts and work for your personal conversion. Brothers and sisters, only in this way will you be able to become witnesses of peace and of the love of God in the world. Open yourselves to prayer so that prayer becomes a need for you. Receive the Love of God, my brothers and sisters, and work so that as many souls as possible may come to know God and His Love. I am close to you and I bless you all. Thank you for having responded to my call.

Message of January 25th, 2002

Dear children! At this time while you are still looking back to the past year I call you, little children, to look deeply into your heart and to decide to be closer to God and to prayer. Little children, you are still attached to earthly things and little to spiritual life. May my call today also be an encouragement to you to decide for God and for daily conversion. You cannot be converted, little children, if you do not abandon sins and do not decide for love towards God and neighbor. Thank you for having responded to my call.

Once again, the modified version:

Dear brothers and sisters! At this time while you are still looking back to the past year I call you, my brothers and sisters, to look deeply into your heart and to decide to be closer to God and to prayer. Brothers and sisters, you are still attached to earthly things and little to spiritual life. May my call today also be an encouragement to you to decide for God and for receiving His Love daily. You cannot receive His Love, brothers and sisters, if you do not abandon sins and do not decide for love towards God and neighbor. Thank you for having responded to my call.

Message to Jacob Colo, 25.12.2001:

Dear Children, today when Jesus is born anew for you, in a special way, I want to call you to conversion. Pray, pray, pray for the conversion of your heart, so that Jesus may be born in you all and may dwell in you and come to reign over your entire being. Thank you for having responded to the call.

Now, the "translation" of this message:

Dear brothers and sisters, today when we commemorate again the bestowal of Divine Love for you, in a special way, I want to call you to receive It. Pray, pray, pray for the New Birth of your heart, so that Christ may be born in you all and may dwell in you and come to reign over your entire being. Thank you for having responded to the call.

Message of December 25th, 2001

Dear children! I call you today and encourage you to prayer for peace. Especially today I call you, carrying the newborn Jesus in my arms for you, to unite with Him through prayer and to become a sign to this peaceless world. Encourage each other, little children, to prayer and love. May your faith be an encouragement to others to believe and to love more. I bless you all and call you to be closer to my heart and to the heart of little Jesus. Thank you for having responded to my call.

And lastly, the Christmas message:

Dear brothers and sisters! I call you today and encourage you to prayer for peace. Especially today I call you, carrying the newborn Jesus in my arms for you, (a catholic symbolism, referring to Christ, that is, the Divine Love) to unite with Him through prayer and to become an example to this peaceless world. Encourage each other, little children, to prayer and love. May your faith be an encouragement to others to believe and to love more. I bless you all and call you to be closer us, your Heavenly guides, and to the Love of the Father. Thank you for having responded to my call.

As you see, we have not selected messages we deem fit, but we have reproduced all the latest messages received in Bosnia.

In practically all the missives, you may see that the central theme is prayer, for the reasons I have explained in our last message. Prayer is the key that opens up, for each individual, the door to greater knowledge of the soul and, of course, in the first place to the Father's Love. What you yesterday thought to be a great novelty, actually we have been preaching all the time.

You can also see that in the above messages, there is constant confusion between Jesus and Christ, because for the Catholics (and not only for them) both words are synonymous. You know that this is not correct at all. However, knowing how to interpret the words, it is simple to find out the intention of the communicating spirit.

If somebody asks you, therefore, if you agree with what has been transmitted in Medjugorje, you can agree with all your heart. The contents of the messages are exactly what we want to impart. The formulation may look questionable, but this should not worry you. And just because of the nitpicking about formulations, about idioms and superficialities, the desire to spread our message suffers great setbacks. Do you understand me now?

Remember that one day, when you were traveling with a friend, you started a conversation with him on the Padgett messages. At first, your friend was very interested, but when you came to explain to him that there was no virgin birth of Jesus, and some other things, your friend immediately raised a complete blockade against the topic, and the conversation suffered a sudden and sad death. Yes, my friend, so it happens. It is easy to hurt the religious feelings of people, and it is so easy to achieve that, which at the beginning looks like an opening up of the soul and a great expectation, suddenly becomes a hopeless barring of the door.

False beliefs do exist, and they will always exist on earth and in the spirit world, as long as there is one single soul that has not been transformed by the Love of God.

Think it over. Do you want to communicate the essence of Truth, or do you want to put an end to false beliefs? Alternatively, do you maybe want to put an end to both things at the same time? Do you believe that you do not hold false beliefs and that you are the owners of the truth and nothing but the truth? You don't believe this? Neither do I. And if you have not managed to put an end by now to all your false beliefs, how do you want to sweep these beliefs of others off this world?

When you find a battered house, what will you do first? Will you make sure that the foundations are stable and fix the roof, so that the rain will not destroy the interior, or will you arm yourself with brush and paint to cover the fine cracks in the walls? First comes the most important thing! And the first step is prayer, a step that eventually will be constantly repeated.

The Truth is that God is Love, and that He offers to share this Love with all of us, when we express through our longings the deep desire of receiving It, for this way to come to at-onement with our Creator. This Truth is enough to save everybody. Let us leave it so.

Before demanding the opening up of others, first open up yourselves. Before preaching, be examples. I repeat, look for what you have in common, build a solid base, and your undertaking will be successful. Now I will definitely conclude this message. We have almost forgotten Jesus and his life in first century Palestine. I would like to soon take up again that series of messages.

May God bless you all, and the Reverend should not worry about false beliefs. What is false, will eventually die, only Truth will remain: Our Father in the Heavens, the God of Love, wishes that we communicate with Him, so that we may enjoy the privilege of living with Him in the mansions of His Eternal Kingdom.

Enjoy a lovely weekend, and receive the Father's blessings,

Your brother in Christ,

Judas

Note. The usage above of the Medjugorje messages is not intended to infringe any copyright that may be asserted by the medium who received those messages.

© Copyright is asserted in this message by Geoff Cutler 2013

Mediumship contributes to the beliefs of others through many different channels and sources. This message is a powerful example of how the mind interprets the message intended to the point of almost being unrecognizable from the original intent. Yet the angels persist in their efforts to teach mortals the truth.

Direct voice is a form of mediumship which bypasses the need to use a medium's brain for transmission. This form of mediumship is called physical mediumship because it uses substances extracted from the human body to form an actual physical transmission device. Most commonly, it works by forming a human voice box out of something called ectoplasm which is an amalgam of a substance drawn from the cells of a human body combined with materials from the spirit side of life. Ectoplasm can be more present in some bodies that are prone to physical manifestations than others who are not.

Physical mediumship is somewhat rare, nor is it easy to develop. The Scole Experimental Group in England has been very successful in the past bringing all manner of manifestations including messages from departed souls transmitted by voice with the spirits own words and language. Spirits such as Winston Churchill have spoken to this group with Direct Voice mediumship. Its great disadvantage is that it requires a darkened room or cabinet to accomplish the connection.

I have recently been part of a group which aspires to bring Celestials through with physical mediumship so that they might speak unencumbered by the limitations of trance mediums. I would be absolutely delighted to be put out of a job as a trance medium and assist in having these magnificent spirits speak to us directly. I believe that this would make the world stand up and take notice if such a thing were possible in the clear light of day. Our guides and teachers say that it is possible but the weak link lies in our lack of higher soul development. It would require a great deal of spiritual power to accomplish this but there are now seven of us willing to try and have committed to this venture. No doubt it will require some time and effort to be accomplished in any tangible way. This is something that we believe the world can benefit from and it also serves as a tool to motivate our personal soul growth. It may never be realized in our lifetime but we fully intend to keep going until someday this gift comes to fruition. It may be that others will take over where we leave off. There are always further challenges and exciting prospects in the realm of mediumship. Never a dull moment!

Chapter 8

Finding our way

Mediumship involves all parts of us on many levels of our being. We are an organic whole that encapsulates our soul which is entirely nonphysical. Our angel friends, who are always working with us, are there to support us in ways that would be almost impossible for us to fully comprehend. We see so little, only the tip of the iceberg and lucky at that to be aware of some of the things that are happening when in close rapport with the Celestials in spirit communication. The angels may indeed come and deliver a message if the group or individual is open to receiving it if a medium is present and in good 'spiritual condition'.

It is unfortunate that there are so few Divine Love mediums in the world and the benefit of receiving a message in group prayer is not at all a common occurrence. Developing Divine Love mediums is an important way to help facilitate more teachings and support from the angels. Divine Love circles tend to be more cohesive and durable when a medium is able to channel communications which support and teach those present. There are thousands, possibly millions of Celestial angels more than willing to work with mortals who are sincerely pursuing the development of our souls through receiving Divine Love. They also make an effort to educate those who are interested in these matters. There is a great need in this regard and an open invitation from those in spirit to help facilitate the development of mediums. The ball then is in our court, but as has been discussed, this development is predicated on a firm grounding in Divine Love. Standards are important too. It is possible for lesser developed spirits to pose as Celestials if the medium is not cautious as we are often seeing through a glass darkly with matters of communication and rapport.

Trance mediumship is a rare and coveted opportunity for spirits to communicate with mortals. Anyone who attempts to open up this and related gifts either because they have an innate ability or wish to direct their energies in this direction will no doubt be noticed by many spirits. The advice given more than once in this book stresses that this venture cannot be taken lightly. It is more of a life's work than a casual side line. How one proceeds requires wisdom, focus, spiritual awareness and a meaningful relationship with the Divine. Anything less than this will more than likely invite communication which is either of a lesser quality or a different order of spirit teachings. We only take those who are strong, as was said to me years ago, is relevant to anyone who seeks to be a Divine Love medium.

To sum up the points made in our discussion on Divine Love mediumship I will list what I believe are key points which will support and encourage your own path towards Divine Love mediumship.

- A strong foundation and dedication in prayer for God's Divine Love is of the utmost importance

- Seeking the highest in prayer, thoughts and intention is the key for success.

- Having a personal, soulful relationship with the Creator follows from a consistent and prayerful connection in receiving God's Divine Love

- A mental diet of higher thoughts combined with acts of love helps to facilitate a strong rapport with the Angels.

- Asking in prayer for the 'Cloak of Protection' from all spirits and influence that are not Celestial can help neutralize possible problems concerning rapport with non-Celestial spirits.

- Pray for soul discernment so that you can recognize what rapport and influence is with you.

- Ask that you may receive a gatekeeper who allows only Celestial spirits through the door of your mediumship.

- Ask that you may be a clear channel of God's Love for others.

- Be loving towards yourself as without a balanced and loving condition within, it is difficult for the Celestials to penetrate our spiritual condition.

- Fostering your own soul growth, including purifying through soul expiation, elevates your soul development thereby facilitating a closer rapport with the angels and allowing higher messages and teachings to come through in your mediumship.

- Always expect and be confident that your efforts resulting in prayer and your desires for the highest will be evident in your gifts

- Understand that this form of mediumship is developed incrementally. Just as the infusion of God's Essence is a gradual and incremental process, so is the opening of the avenues of communication with the Angels.

- It is important to realize that no medium is perfect and no medium is identical in gifts and abilities to another medium. Therefore, do not compare yourself with others. It is not helpful or practical to do so.

- Always be consistent and focused with your prayers and intentions.

- Do not indulge in negative thoughts and actions towards others or towards yourself. This will distance you from the angels as it causes diminishment of your light.

- The more consistent you are with living the Laws of Divine Love through prayer, thought and action, the greater and easier will be your rapport with the Celestial angels.

- Never enter into a negative condition unless your intention is to bring it to a place of change for the better.

- Try to live a life that is grounded and balanced. The angels do not expect you to be in a perpetual state of unearthly rapport with them. They respect and honor our needs to live our material lives, as this also provides us with essential avenues for spiritual growth.

- Understand that life is always changing and your gifts will deepen and evolve with time. Soul growth through receiving Divine Love ensures that this development will take place.

- Trust your intuition. If something does not feel right when delivering a message, say a prayer to close the session. At some future date it would be advisable to ask for clarification of the situation from your guides.

- Not every message will be clear and perfect. Error and confusing information can come through the most well intentioned and developed medium. Mediumship is more art than science. Do not judge yourself as being ineffective or unworthy as a medium if the results are not as expected. The earth plane is a very imperfect and often spiritually hostile environment. We are all susceptible to dark conditions and sometimes they get the better of us. Best to not dwell on recent failures and cultivate a positive attitude for success. The angels will never criticize or be hurtful towards budding mediums. Their approach is patient and loving. If they do point out a problem, it is because they are particularly concerned about a turn of direction or attitude that you may have taken. Everything they communicate is done in love and in the interests of harmony. If you do not see this to be the case, then question the source. If no reasonable explanation is given, then it is safe to assume that either you are unable to hear the truth of the matter or the truth is not present in the explanation.

- Be humble. Remember that you are merely the conduit or instrument for spirit to communicate through you. Though it is a noble act on your part, it is far less complex and difficult than what the angels do in order to establish the link between you and them. Though you are profoundly blessed to be able to be a part of this process, you are always the weakest link in the chain. The angels come a very great distance, from the Celestial Heavens, in order to connect with mortals. Never assume that what is conveyed in their countenance and rapport with you reflects on your own light and condition. In truth, we are dim flames of spiritual light compared to their starburst of soul Love.

- Remember, there is a plan that is carefully orchestrated by the angels and blessed by God. To have a role to play in the unfolding of God's plan for the salvation of humanity is a great blessing. Being used as an instrument of light, bringing truth to others is a gift of profound importance that will bring many blessings and experiences to you. Be joyful in your work and have faith that there is indeed purpose, great comfort and healing for others in using your gifts in this way.

In closing I wish to share this message received through me from our beloved Teacher and angel friend Augustine, encouraging us in our work and fellowship together. It is in these words one realizes the depth and beauty of this work. We will be blessed ten times over is his pronouncement regarding our spiritual work. I believe that anyone who is truly committed to serve humanity and be guided by God in so doing will receive these blessings. It is work that is waiting for any and all who are willing. The present state of our world indicates that time is running short for humanity. We are all facing a wakeup call regarding the dreadful state of our planet. For those who are willing to take up the torch for change and spiritual awakening, God's Hand will surely guide us. Augustine, who was the Bishop of Hippo in the year 300 AD, urges us forward.

Spirit: Augustine July 15th, 2018

> *I am your teacher Augustine. All those who commit to doing this work shall receive the blessings and support of the Angels. How few there are in this world, who are willing to step forward in this way. How few are prepared to engage in this great task of bringing the truth of God's Love to the world in ways and means that are clear and loving and*

consistent. How precious are all of you, beloved souls, who have committed your soul to seeking at-onement with God through His Love.

Any efforts that you may make to be a channel of blessings for others, to bring greater light to this world, and greater truth, are indeed blessed. For any small effort you make, you are blessed ten times over by God. This is the generosity of God's Love for you, beloved souls, that whatever you may do, even in prayer, is blessed mightily by God. Indeed your souls are well aware of this and are motivated greatly by this knowledge, that whatever efforts you make are indeed blessed. Even when there are those who combine error with this truth, there is some blessing, some benefit. So I would urge you not to judge those whom you do not agree with in their perspective, and yet, as with you, they pray for the Father's Love to enter their souls. And as with you, they will grow, their knowledge will grow, their perspective will change, their love will flow.

Continue in these efforts beloved souls, and all who wish to serve God in this way will indeed have the blessings of angels by their side. For there is a great effort afoot to bring the conditions of change to this world, that will bring greater light and truth, love and harmony. This must be so. It is important at this time that there is a concerted effort on your part and others, to bring this truth forward.

Your world is in jeopardy. Your world suffers greatly. There is such error and confusion. So much of the energies of mankind are placed upon material efforts, neglecting the balance that is needed for the spiritual to be awakened, the wisdom of your souls to govern your actions. So beloveds, you are asked to be a living example of the power of God's Love within your soul. You work diligently to try to make this a truth within you, to bring the wisdom forth, to walk in light, to be a channel of love. We walk with you as you well know. So much yet to be discovered, so much more wisdom to come forward, and greater love always, to be expressed.

It is indeed a journey of awakening that comes with each day. You are drawn together in prayer with one another, and discussions and expressions of love. God makes it possible for you to have these times of nurturing together so that you may learn from one another, and grow, and reinforce the bonds of love that are important. For it is in the power of these bonds of love that you share comes the flow, the clarity of light that nurtures you all. For as one steps forward, so you all step forward. As one awakens a little more, so do you all. For this is shared within this great bond and flow of Love.

Be inspired by one another, my beloveds. Pray for one another. Realize that within these bonds that you share, and the many that also are a part of this community, there is a great resource, a powerful influence for light that you may benefit from, that you may benefit others with, and that together you may benefit the world. This is all part of God's plan, that you all walk in this world as brothers and sisters, connected in love, awakened in love.

May God bless you mightily my beloved, beloved souls. May you continue to walk upon this path of love and share your journeys together. So much awaits you on this journey, as you help one another to clear the barriers. For do you not understand that from your own experiences and struggles each must go through to clear this path? In this deep compassion and awareness lies a great strength that you may rely upon with each other. Do not hesitate to be open and vulnerable, clear and truthful with one another. For this engenders more love and more light.

God bless you beloveds. I am your teacher Augustine. I love you, I see your light, I mark your progress and I will continue to walk with you for all eternity. This is my commitment to you. I will be your friend, your guide and teacher for all eternity. You may rely upon my efforts and wisdom to help you along your journey. We all walk towards at-onement with God. God bless you, beloveds, God bless you

It is my sincere hope that those who have read this book have been inspired to pursue the development of their gifts. We all possess a great reservoir of abilities and wisdom within us. It is the gift of receiving God's Divine Love that unlocks the treasure chest of our souls. No matter our position in life, our past experiences or misdeeds, God is waiting to relieve you of your burdens and bring you to a place of joy and peace. In this journey we are all compelled to reach out to our brothers and sisters the world over. If you have mediumistic abilities and they are developed through the avenue of soul awakening, the potential of what you may do to assist many who are seeking is truly without limitations. This path is both exhilarating and challenging, but without life experiences such as these, we blend into the fabric of humanity and are lost in the human condition. If you are willing to stand out from the crowd and live a life of service predicated on Love, then what is proposed here may propel you on a journey like none other.

May God bless all who are brave enough, strong enough and have a deep desire to teach truth in service to humanity. The world needs all who are willing to discover and express their full potential. May you be awakened to this call and find your unique road in the expression of your gifts of the soul.

Further References

Websites:

Http://divinelovesanctuary.com

http://board.divine-love-sanctuary.ca

http://new-birth.net

http://www.fcdt.org

http://www.divinelove.org

Related books:

"True Gospel Revealed Anew by Jesus" Vol. I, II, III and IV by James Padgett

Available from divinelove.org and fcdt.org and Amazon Kindle bookstore, and new-birth.net

"Judas of Kerioth", available on Amazon /Kindle bookstore and new-birth.net

"The Quiet Revolution of the Soul" by Al Fike available on Amazon and Kindle. This was the first book in this series,

and concentrates on sharing how to grow in the Divine Love.

Numerous Divine Love publications by Joseph Babinsky available on Lulu